GOLD MEDAL SELLING

GOLD MEDAL SELLING

Ten Conditioning Strategies for World-Class Performance

Paperback: 978-0-578-66235-0

E-book: 978-0-578-66236-7

CONTENTS

ACKNOWLEDGMENTS

WE ACKNOWLEDGE the countless clients and colleagues who shared lessons and insights that shaped what went into these pages.

FOREWORD

GREAT SALESPEOPLE are like great athletes in many ways, but this book spotlights the most important similarity: They are relentlessly committed to conditioning.

David Sandler, the founder of our firm, once noted that "Conditioning is a way of life"—not just for successful salespeople, but for successful professionals in all disciplines. Sandler went on to define conditioning as "a set of rules, sometimes philosophical, but always practical" that those who become top performers, and who remain at the top year after year, find a way to follow on a daily basis. They make this daily commitment in order to ensure their success within their chosen field. This book identifies ten of those daily rules for salespeople and connects each of them to the story of a celebrated Olympic athlete. It's an enduring reminder of the extraordinary power of conditioning, in sales as in every other field of human endeavor.

Gold medals don't just happen. They are the result of long periods of training, endless repetition of the fundamentals, and an ongoing, relentless emphasis on identifying and living the right behaviours, the right attitudes, and the right techniques. If you or someone on your team aspires to the sales equivalent of a gold medal, this book was written for you.

David Mattson
President/CEO, Sandler Training

INTRODUCTION

The Process That Leads to Gold Medal Selling

THIS BOOK is all about achieving at the highest possible level in the field of selling—the level we at Sandler call "gold medal selling." The question people always ask is whether there is a process that someone who is new to sales can follow to achieve at this level. The answer we give—"Yes"—often surprises. Let us explain why we are so confident in that answer.

Sandler has helped tens of thousands of salespeople become more effective sales professionals and perform at levels they would once have considered not just unrealistic, but literally impossible. More than one of these clients has told us that the Sandler process helped them take their game to a world-class level, a level of performance akin to that of a superstar athlete.

This started a conversation at Sandler about how the process-driven regimen of the Olympic athlete is comparable to the process-driven regimen of the most successful salespeople. Thus the idea for this book was born.

What process supports gold medal performance in the field of sales? The chapters that follow attempt to answer that question. Our aim is to spread the word and to help those who are tired of achieving average (or worse) sales results to move up to the level of the gold medal performer.

In this book, we'll be talking a lot about two very different types of salesperson: the gold medal salesperson and the amateur salesperson. The twin comparisons with Olympic-level achievement and with a less committed interest in a given sport is intentional. Of course, technically, some Olympic champions are not professional athletes, but even so, this distinction is worth making because it sums up the dichotomy that plays out in the world of sales time and time again: Amateurs are not committed to conditioning, and superior salespeople are. So when you see the word "amateur," think "someone who isn't committed to conditioning."

A Gold Medal Skill Set?

Here's a question. How much specialised training would you estimate the very best Olympic athletes must put in to even earn a spot on their country's national team? The answer varies by country and by specialty, but it is always measured in years and sometimes even in decades.

Now, how much sales training do most salespeople get before they start competing on behalf of their company? Often there is zero specialised training—or, if the salespeople are lucky, they may get a couple of days at a seminar. Isn't that incredible? Other than whatever it is a business manages to produce, surely the most important part of any business is sales. Yet most salespeople are not (by any reasonable standard) trained sales professionals. *They have not put in the training time.*

Most salespeople, truth be told, start out as amateurs, in the worst sense of that word. This highlights one of the major topics of this book: the difference between gold medal salespeople and amateur salespeople. That difference can be summed up in a single word familiar to anyone who follows sports: conditioning.

Many people play sports. In all sports there are both amateur athletes and professional athletes. Obviously, only a very small proportion wind up being professional. How do each of these two types of athletes behave? Amateur athletes tend to approach their sport in a more ad hoc fashion—they practice and play when they want to and generally are average (or worse) in terms of their results when compared to the very best in their field. Professional athletes, by contrast, are highly focused. They follow well-defined practice routines, and they achieve exceptional results compared to amateur athletes.

Are All Sales "Gyms" Equal?

Many sales leaders find themselves looking around for training and support for their team. What they find are sales systems that are technique-based and generally built around one- or two-day courses. These sales approaches can provide some short-term improvement to results, but very rarely do they turn amateurs into professionals.

Sending salespeople to one of those courses is a lot like amateurs occasionally going to the gym and just doing the basics. Long-term, sustainable improvement is unlikely. There has to be a better way. Indeed, there is.

Welcome to the Sandler® sales gym. This is where gold medal salespeople are born.

The Sandler Selling System® methodology is like a holistic, all-encompassing "sales gym" that emphasises conditioning on the same scale and with the same intensity as that adopted by the world's best athletes.

Unlike most traditional sales training, which focuses almost exclusively on technique in order to achieve sales success, the Sandler system works with three interrelated factors: behaviour, attitude, and technique. Behaviour relates to having a systematic approach for reaching sales goals—"muscle memory," if you will. Attitude has to do with your outlook. Technique consists of the tactics and strategies you put into practice. Using all three of these interrelated factors, you have a much greater opportunity for sales success. All of these will be covered in this book.

The sales gym also provides ongoing reinforcement and support. This is another reason that working out at the sales gym consistently creates long-lasting sales performance improvement.

Here at the sales gym, you'll learn to work with the three sales muscles groups—behaviour, attitude, and technique—and the 10 most important sales muscles. If you work to improve them, you will be well on the road to achieving at the gold medal level.

Based on the Sandler system, this book offers a proven 10-point programme that enables salespeople to develop as professionals and take guidance from the way Olympic athletes train and perform. *NOTE*: Building your "sales muscle" requires training and ongoing reinforcement at the Sandler sales gym. This book is only a start, but nothing good happens without a start, does it?

On your mark...get set...go!

SALES MUSCLE #1

What You Believe Becomes Your Reality

"Worrying gets you nowhere. If you turn up worrying about how you're going to perform, you've already lost. Train hard, turn up, run your best, and the rest will take care of itself."

—USAIN BOLT

USAIN BOLT, an eight-time Olympic gold medalist, is the first to hold simultaneous world records in both the men's 100-metre and 200-metre categories since automatic time measurements became mandatory in 1977, a feat that places him at the pinnacle of human athletic endeavor. He is a believer, both in his faith (Catholicism) and in himself. During his extraordinary career, he was widely acknowledged for his extraordinary confidence, trusting in abilities rooted in years of training, to hone both his physiology and his finely tuned motor skills. When Bolt got ready to run a race, he had good reason to believe that he had prepared harder and longer than anyone else on that track.

Bolt had a clear strategy that he followed with great discipline in each and every race. In the 100-metre event, for instance, he divided the race into sections and pursued a distinct process for each. In the first half of the race, he began racing tall and upright out of the blocks. At 50 metres, he gave himself the opportunity to glance left and right to check his placement amongst his competitors. Most crucially, 10 metres from the finish line Bolt locked in beliefs he had earned from years of conditioning, assuring himself with an internal soliloquy aimed at his competitors: "You are not going to catch me. It doesn't matter who you are. It doesn't matter what you are doing."

That internal monologue confirmed a deep, unshakeable belief in his own potential. Kindling that belief into a roaring flame is a hallmark of gold medal athletes, and it is a hallmark of gold medal salespeople as well. Such self-assurance isn't arrogance, and it isn't misplaced. Gold medal performers earn this belief through dedication and persistence. They realise it doesn't happen automatically or by accident. They commit to instilling a healthy belief in their own potential and strengthening it each and every day with constant conditioning and a devotion to the ideal of learning more, practicing more, and executing at a higher level than ever before. That's what makes them champions.

Amateurs vs. Gold Medal Salespeople

Amateur salespeople tend to think that reality is a fixed concept. Some of them feel that what happens to them is not really within their control and that they are purely or mostly victims of circumstance. These amateur salespeople say things like: "It's a tough market out there," or "Gatekeepers are keeping me from getting through to senior decision makers." After events confirm their self-fulfilling prophecies, they feel they have evidence of these truths. They then make this their reality. "I just can't get past gatekeepers!" they cry. Surprise, surprise—this is what happens from that moment forward.

Gold medal salespeople, by contrast, do not let outside circumstances deter them from anything, including prospecting. Whether gatekeepers hang up, prospects tell them never to call back, or a deal that is about to be signed falls through, they assume that reality is up to them to define. External factors do not affect the self-belief of the gold medal sales professional.

The truth is that salespeople are responsible for their attitude and behaviour—and yes, their own reality—no matter what happens. The professional salesperson knows that the control and creation of a belief system is up to them. This in turn impacts directly on the results achieved.

All the thoughts in your head, whether helpful or unhelpful, are just opinions that you have come to accept as true. The only real truth is that what you think will determine what you see and perceive as reality—and what you feel as a result. You have control of your attitude, which means you, like Usain Bolt, have control of your reality.

The Science behind Attitude

Your attitude, meaning your outlook on yourself, your life, and the world, comes directly from your beliefs. The thoughts that you hold dear are formed as a result of your life experiences and what you have been taught since you were a child. The trick is to start noticing this.

Both gold medal athletes and gold medal salespeople understand the theory of belief systems. They have put this theory into practice to improve their performance by means of a system known as creative visualisation. They learn to see themselves doing whatever is necessary to succeed—before they actually do it.

The Self-Fulfilling Prophecy: What You Believe Creates Your Reality

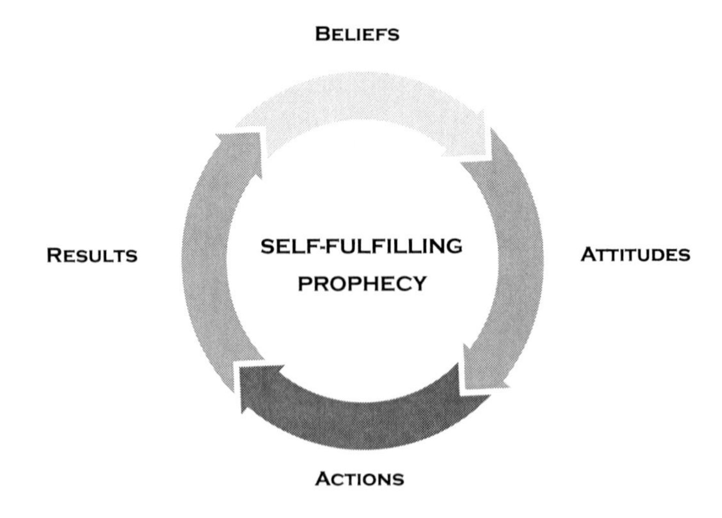

The model above is known as the Belief Wheel. It is a reminder that your beliefs determine your attitude. Think again of what Usain Bolt recites in the final 10 metres of a race: "You are not going to catch me. It doesn't matter who you are. It doesn't matter what you are doing."

So how does this distinguish gold medal salespeople from amateurs? To give just one example, gold medal salespeople always believe that they will hit their quarterly sales targets consistently. Because they have such a strong and powerful belief, they have an attitude of supreme confidence. This translates to how they interact with their prospects.

What's more, gold medal salespeople are willing to follow a consistent weekly prospecting plan, composed of mixed sales activities, to ensure positive results. These sales professionals have a steadfast belief in themselves, and this belief determines the attitude and manner in which their actions are performed. The outcome is behaviour that supports the targeted results.

Fake It Until You Make It

Not everyone can be the world's fastest human. No one can close every deal. However, you are responsible for believing in yourself and for fulfilling your own potential to achieve. That's something you have in common with Usain Bolt.

The difference between being an amateur performer and a gold medal salesperson is acting like an A-Player. An A-Player accepts that it is the individual's responsibility to get the very most out of their abilities. Moreover, A-Players take control of their beliefs and behaviours and act to become the best version of who they can be. This is how you can achieve your goals as both a salesperson and in all aspects of your life. But here's the problem: You can't expect to achieve important goals unless you understand what you already believe—and why.

Your First Five Years

Your core beliefs were formed during the first five years of your life, and they generally come from your primary caregivers. (Of course, they also grow to include other factors such as culture, country, religion, and all other life experiences that you encounter.)

You were like a sponge during those first five years, and the beliefs that you imbibed then became hard-coded. Even now, you view your reality through these beliefs. These beliefs became entrenched in your psyche and determine your attitude and drive as an adult. Moreover, they influence what you are willing to do—and what you are not willing to do.

Your reality, your experiences of life (including your sales results), are no more than a reflection of your beliefs—and those beliefs are not even entirely yours. They were what you heard and absorbed in the first five years of your life.

Most people have been taught lessons as children that turned out to not benefit them as adults, including salespeople. When you were very young, were you told, "Go speak to as many strangers as possible"? No, of course not. You were told, "Don't speak to strangers." How does that make you feel about, say, phone prospecting?

You may also have been told, "Money doesn't grow on trees." How does that make you feel about talking to prospects about how much they need to pay you to benefit from working with you? How likely are you to want to offer a discount? Money is hard to come by, after all.

These are just two examples of what you heard growing up. Your belief systems could be affecting your sales performance now as an adult.

Two Kinds of Beliefs

Empowering beliefs are positive and support your actions. If you believe that your company has a great product and that your marketplace is in dire need of your services, as a salesperson you are likely to want to pick up the phone and prospect immediately and with great vigor. You won't let the occasional grouchy gatekeeper affect your confidence. This is because you believe that your prospects are going to be grateful and happy as a result of your persistence when they do buy from you.

Disempowering beliefs, in contrast, cultivate a negative attitude and make you feel more anxious about taking action. A common fear for many salespeople, for example, is the worry, "I won't hit my sales numbers this month." When this is the case, if a prospect says, "I'm not interested," the amateur salesperson's response is fear. This is because the amateur salesperson translates this response into thinking that very few people will buy the product or that the goods or services being sold are not worth buying.

The outcome and resulting reality reinforces these fears. It's safe to say that if salespeople believe these disempowering ideas wholeheartedly, it is unlikely that they will hit their monthly numbers. The system explained in this book defines such disempowering beliefs as "head trash." Head trash includes all limiting thoughts that go round and round in your head.

So, let's go back to the Belief Wheel. When it comes to beliefs, you can have an outlook of limitations or an outlook of possibilities. It's all about what you choose. Professional salespeople, much like Usain Bolt, choose an outlook of possibilities. They then implement empowering beliefs to reflect and strengthen this choice.

If you are willing to challenge and change your disempowering beliefs, then there will be a corresponding change in your results.

Clara's Story

When we first met Clara, she was struggling as a marketing consultant. She worked very long hours and believed that it was a tough market out there. She charged a daily rate of £500 (US$645) and was constantly being beaten up on rates. We told her that her pricing was too low. Moreover, she was attracting penny-pinching clients who did not value her. She found this hard to swallow. When we then recommended that she increase her daily rate to £1,500, she nearly fell over.

Clara held the disempowering belief that she could not charge any more than £500 per day for her services. Not only did she believe that people would not pay her that fee and selling at that level would be difficult, but also she believed her services were not worth more than £500 and that she did not deserve to earn any more than that. These beliefs led her to a mental state of constant stress and depression, and they supported a behaviour pattern we would describe as "desperate." Basically, she was under such financial and emotional stress that she would take any meeting, with anyone, at any time—even with someone who was manifestly unqualified to be a prospect.

We slowly helped Clara to discover new empowering beliefs that helped her change both her business and her life. Two of her new beliefs were: "The market does not dictate what I charge for my services," and "I provide incredible value for the services that I deliver, and I charge accordingly."

It did not happen overnight, but slowly and surely Clara was willing to challenge her old head trash. Now, three years later, her daily rate is over £3,000 per day—and she has a very impressive new client base. Her clients are happy to pay her what she deserves.

Good News and Bad News

The good news is that your disempowering beliefs can be changed. The bad news is that it takes effort and a determined willingness to move through your comfort zones.

First, identify your disempowering beliefs. When you are undertaking sales activities, be aware of your negative thoughts throughout the day and write them down—not to reinforce them, but to help you notice how absurd they are. Next, visualise yourself achieving your sales goals for the month, happily doing all you need to do to achieve them. Your head trash will become more noticeable and will eventually recede.

You know you need to make some cold calls. The next thought that probably comes to mind is, "People don't want to hear from me," or "The people I speak to are going to be rude and will tell me to go away." If you allow a dominant negative thought to stay with you, you are likely to resist the action of making cold calls. This is pure head trash.

It is important to realise that your beliefs are just thoughts in your head and can't be proved to be true or untrue—until you have experienced them to be so in life. However, as discussed earlier, what you believe will happen tends to happen. When you have identified an example of sales head trash, such as, "I am fearful of people telling me to get lost," take control and create a new empowering belief that is 180 degrees different from your head-trash belief.

For the head trash above, the new empowering belief could

be: "The service that I have to offer is of great value, but it is OK for some people to tell me that they are not interested." Or, "My product is amazing—and it's their lucky day to get a call from me!"

Exercise: Taking Out Your Head Trash

Head trash is nothing more than holding an outlook of limiting thoughts and disempowering beliefs. To overcome this, write down the empowering belief that is the opposite of your head trash.

When we do this exercise with salespeople in our Sandler sales gym, the result usually looks something like the following.

Your Head Trash	Your Empowering Beliefs
"I'm not good enough."	"I am more than good enough."
"I might fail."	"Every time I fail I am one step closer to success."
Company Head Trash	**Company Empowering Beliefs**
"Our company is too small."	"Clients love the personal service our small company provides."
Marketplace Head Trash	**Marketplace Empowering Beliefs**
"There are not enough good prospects."	"There is an endless supply of prospects."
"Potential clients mess me around."	"I only work with clients I like and respect."

Do the exercise above before you move on to the next chapter. Once you do, you will have started working out your first sales muscle. Developing this muscle is a core behaviour of gold medal salespeople.

Reflection

What you believe becomes your reality. Actions are required to achieve results, but all your actions are driven by attitude. Amateur salespeople do not understand the science of how to build a powerful attitude, and thus both their attitude and actions are generally erratic and inconsistent. In contrast, professional salespeople recognise that they need a winning attitude, and this can be achieved by working on their belief system.

SALES MUSCLE #2

Learn What Makes People Tick

"Enduring means accepting. Accepting things as they are and not as you would wish them to be, and then looking ahead, not behind."

—RAFAEL NADAL

SUPERSTAR RAFAEL NADAL, in addition to winning the 2008 Olympic gold medal in singles tennis and the Olympic gold for men's doubles in 2016, has won 19 Grand Slam singles titles, the second most in history for a male player. He has also won 35 ATP Tour Masters 1000 titles (another record) and 20 ATP Tour 500 titles. He has, as this book goes to press, held the world ranking as top male tennis player for a total of

196 weeks, including being the year-end #1 four times. Nadal has won a record twelve French Open titles, four U.S. Open titles, two Wimbledon titles and one Australian Open title. He was a member of the winning Spain Davis Cup team in 2004, 2008, 2009, and 2011. And you know what? He's not done yet. By the time you read these words, he may well have added something new and astonishing to his extraordinary list of accomplishments on the court. By any measure, the man is a true champion in his chosen field, and one of the greatest ever to play the game of tennis. And his physical skills are astonishing.

But physical conditioning is not what this chapter is about. It's about another kind of conditioning entirely. That's because there is something besides his undeniable physical prowess that separates Nadal from so many of the other champions of his sport. We are talking about an internal difference here.

Rafael Nadal has mastered the mental game, and as a direct result of that mastery, he is a true gentleman.

It's not that other tennis stars are incapable of gentlemanly (or gentlewomanly) behaviour. Rather, Nadal understands himself and others, and as a result of that understanding, he always approaches the game he loves as a grownup, not as a child, and with an accompanying laser-like focus. Although he faces any number of players with comparable or even superior physical skills, few if any of the opponents who play at his level are as good at the mental game as he is. (Nadal's September 2019 defeat of the much younger Daniil Medvedev at the

U.S. Open, in a five-hour match for the ages, is proof enough of that.)

Nadal has a great reputation among his peers, not just because of his skills on the court, but because of his ability to sustain mental and emotional balance. He is unfailingly polite. Period. Rudeness is simply not a part of his game. That may sound like a simple thing, being polite, but it's important to understand that this doesn't mean being falsely polite and inauthentic. It means treating people with true respect, and meaning what you say and do in the process. That takes some doing, and some practice, in a hypercompetitive environment like the world of world-class tennis and also in the hypercompetitive world of business. There are jerks out there. Authentic politeness doesn't happen by accident in either realm.

True politeness, the kind of politeness that goes beyond surface posturing, requires three things: effective peer-to-peer communication, self-awareness, and the ability to manage one's own emotional responses at the same time you're dealing with the responses of others.

No one is born with these skills. People need to learn them and practice them and perfect them over time. Anyone who has carefully watched Nadal play in even one of his high-pressure matches cannot escape the conclusion that he is a master at all three skills. It is not easy to establish a mature, nonjudgmental path of interaction with opponents, officials, and others, to keep a handle on your own emotions, and to decline the countless opportunities for toxic drama that arise during a big match. But Nadal never seems to get caught up in the drama. And it is that ability to rise above that drama that allows him to sustain the extraoardinary mental focus that has served as the foundation of his remarkable accomplishments in tennis. This ability to rise above the drama is the result of conditioning.

To rise above the drama—not once in a while, but consistently; not by accident, but as a matter of conscious choice, and not just on the job, but everywhere else in your life—requires a special kind of understanding that is only developed over time. It requires an understanding of what makes people tick. Rafael Nadal has that kind of understanding. Gold medal salespeople have it, too. In this chapter, you get a remarkable opportunity: the opportunity to gain the same level of understanding and put it to work in support of your own career as a salesperson, and indeed in all your relationships.

It won't happen overnight. This chapter may take a half an hour or so to read, but it will take a good deal longer than that to master. It will take repetition. It will take practice. It will take conditioning. So give yourself as much time as you need. Come back to this chapter as often as necessary, and put its ideas into practice over and over again in the weeks and months ahead. If you do that, you will eventually find yourself joining the ranks of the true masters of the mental game, like Rafael Nadal.

So let's get down to it. An important psychological theory known as the theory of transactional analysis (TA for short) is a very effective human-relations model for understanding how and why professional salespeople, their clients, and their prospects behave as they do. TA is the key to figuring out what makes people tick. Nadal has probably never heard of TA. But just from watching him play—watching him create personal routines that support him and keep him focused; watching him take account of his own strengths and weaknesses and somehow always find ways to maximise the former and work around the latter; watching him maintain mindfulness and total composure over the course of a long match without ever taking things personally; watching him keep all his interactions on an adult-to-adult level—all of that says he'd be very, very good at coaching other people on this stuff. Wouldn't it be great to sit in on that seminar? Until he takes that task on for you, though, you can learn more about TA here.

What Is TA?

Transactional analysis was developed by psychologist Dr. Eric Berne in the late 1950s. He developed TA when he noticed that his patients, and indeed all people, could and would change over the course of a single conversation. The changes were both verbal and non-verbal, including facial expressions, body language, body temperature, and other cues.

Berne's breakthrough came when he was counselling a 35-year-old lawyer. The two were discussing something the lawyer had done that he had regretted doing. Berne asked him:

"Why then did you do it?" The lawyer explained that, although part of him hadn't wanted to do what he'd done, "the child inside me made me do it."

Berne was inspired. Out of this conversation he developed the TA psychological model. Berne theorised that three influences live within each person: the ego states of the Parent, the Child, and the Adult.

Let's look at each of these in depth.

The Parent Ego State

The Parent ego state acts like an audio recorder, storing lessons and messages people received from their parents and other authority figures from birth until they were about six. This recording cannot be erased.

Sometimes, those messages were communicated in a stern, authoritarian, critical manner (Critical Parent). Examples of recordings in the Critical Parent include: "Never talk to strangers," and "How many times have I told you not to do that?"

At other times those messages were communicated in a more nurturing manner (Nurturing Parent) as helpful suggestions and supportive words. Examples of recordings in the Nurturing Parent include: "You always try your best, and that is always good enough," and "Don't worry that you made a mistake today. You can always learn a lesson when you make a mistake."

These Parent recordings play back at different times in a person's life after the age of five, and they become beliefs that the person then creates within themselves. For adults, these lessons/messages are usually stored as "what-to-do's"—right/wrong, do/don't, should/shouldn't—and largely control judgments and behaviour.

These judgments and behaviours are triggered when adults are faced with something that reminds them of how their parents or other parental figures acted or how they interpreted their parents' actions.

The Adult Ego State

The Adult ego state starts recording at about nine months, continues to record throughout people's entire lives, and filters all the information they receive. People behave, feel, and think in response to what is going on in the present, using all of their resources as an adult human being with their years of life experience to guide them.

The Adult ego state is always rational and analytical and updates information as it is received. It includes two additional elements: the Updated Parent and the Updated Child (for a discussion of the Child ego state, see below).

As the name suggests, the Updated Parent allows people to upgrade the warnings they heard in childhood from the Critical Parent. For example, warnings like, "Don't talk to strangers." Through the Updated Parent, people can update those belief systems and change the way they think about things. For instance, an updated "Don't talk to strangers" belief might be:

"Most people I meet are friendly and interesting, they want to engage with me, and they are eager to talk about themselves. It's exciting to speak to new people, and when I do I generally uncover new opportunities." In a similar way, the Updated Child allows people to update the way they feel about things.

The Child Ego State

The Child ego state is also a recorder that is activated at birth and turns off at about age six. Here are all the feelings that have ever festered inside of a person in response to the ancient Parent recordings: the rights and wrongs, the shoulds and shouldn'ts, and the do's and don'ts that Mom, Dad, and other caregivers were speaking, shouting, or commanding.

This inner voice of the Child cannot be erased, but, like the Parent recordings, people can choose to update it with more empowering and positive messages that then translate into new belief systems.

The Child ego state has four components:

- Adaptive Child: Longing to please the Parent recordings and always seeking approval.
- Rebellious Child: Angry and fearful, often selfish, and always ready and waiting for a fight.
- Natural Child: Playful and creative, uninhibited and spontaneous, and likes fun and laughter.
- Little Professor (combination of Rebellious and Natural

Child): Very manipulative to meet its own needs and not very authentic.

How Does TA Apply in the Sales World?

TA is a model for understanding how salespeople, their clients, and their prospects behave. This is vitally important in sales since sales is always a relationship between at least two people, sometimes one to one, sometimes one to many, or even many to many.

Sales interactions are described as transactions (human relations). The goal is to achieve win-win transactions that create equal business stature, rather than indulging in game-playing that does not create trust. Using TA, win-win transactions occur when each person comes from the Nurturing Parent and Adult ego states.

Sales is not for the faint-hearted. Challenges such as a prospect delaying a sale, a customer making excessive demands, or a client who criticises every step of the sales process are just some of the obstacles salespeople face on a daily basis. When used mindfully, TA can be applied to all your communications with clients and prospects to build effective sales interactions and optimise your sales performance.

Amateur salespeople are unaware or unwilling to implement the TA model and are thus very reactive to challenging situations because they can trigger reverting into a less useful ego state like Critical Parent or Child, which results in wasted time and energy, lost productivity, and generally average sales results. Gold medal salespeople understand that TA enables them to deal effectively with challenging situations, and they put that understanding to work.

Optimal Effective Communication in TA

The optimal effective communication in TA is for a person to come from the Nurturing Parent and Adult ego states as frequently as possible. Ideally, 70% of effective communication comes from the Nurturing Parent and 30% is from the Adult ego state.

In regard to the other ego states, it's often recommended that you leave the Child in the car* and send the Critical Parent on a one-way ticket to outer space.

Strokes

When you come from Nurturing Parent first, you give what are called "strokes" to the person with whom you are communicating.

According to TA, people need daily strokes in order to feel good about themselves. This can be better understood by imagining that someone who did not receive enough physical affection (like hugs and kisses from a loving parent) is generally

* Source: David Sandler.

not going to feel as good about themselves. As professionals in a workplace, however, it is not appropriate to seek physical strokes from others. Stroking needs are satisfied by receiving recognition or approval. Examples of Nurturing Parent strokes are, "I really enjoy working with you," "Great question; I am glad you asked that," etc.

Let's consider two common sales scenarios.

Scenario 1

Early on in the sales process, the prospect demands a proposal before having been properly or thoroughly qualified. The salesperson feels pushed into a features-and-benefits presentation.

Amateur Salesperson Interaction

The amateur salesperson is triggered to go into the Adaptive Child ego state by becoming a people-pleaser. This allows the prospect to take control of the sales process. The prospect usually takes on a Critical Parent ego state. Note that a classic trait of the Critical Parent ego state is telling someone else what to do!

Prospect: "Look. Stop asking me so many questions. Just send me a proposal by Friday with a solution that solves all my problems." (Critical Parent)

Amateur Salesperson: "Oh, well, I'm sorry. Can't I just ask you a few more questions?" (Adaptive Child)

Prospect: "How many times do I have to tell you? Just send me the proposal! Then I will make a decision." (Critical Parent)

Amateur Salesperson (acquiescing): "Of course. I will send you a proposal. You will have it by Friday." (Adaptive Child)

The result of this conversation is that the prospect will be mysteriously unavailable to provide feedback on the proposal once submitted.

Gold Medal Salesperson Interaction

The gold medal salesperson is mindful not to react to the Critical Parent ego state of the prospect. This salesperson handles this challenging scenario by choosing to respond to the prospect in the Nurturing Parent/Adult ego state. This results in the prospect moving back into the Nurturing Parent/Adult ego state. This allows for a win-win or no-deal sales process to continue.

Prospect: "Look. Stop asking me so many questions. Just send me a proposal by Friday with a solution that solves all my problems." (Critical Parent)

Gold Medal Salesperson: "I'd love to potentially send you a proposal. But we can't necessarily help everybody, so I'm going to need to spend a few minutes first so I can really understand exactly what you are looking for, what your investment criteria are, and who the other relevant stakeholders are. Once I have all that information, then I will be able to put together a proposal that really hits the mark. Are you OK with that?" (Nurturing Parent /Adult)

Prospect: "Well, I guess that makes sense." (Nurturing Parent/Adult)

The gold medal salesperson maintains equal business stature by having taken control of the structure of the sales process, which means that this person will only present solutions when the prospect is properly qualified. This ensures there will be mutually-agreed-upon next steps to move the prospect towards a *yes/no* close in a timely fashion.

Scenario 2

At any time in the sales process prospects may suddenly say (sometimes with a great deal of stress in their voice) that the salesperson is presenting outrageous pricing. This is more often than not just a power-play by the prospect.

Amateur Salesperson Interaction

The amateur salesperson feels very uncomfortable in this type of situation, gets triggered into an Adaptive Child ego state, and reacts by trying to placate the prospect and to over-justify the pricing. This actually encourages the prospect to go stronger into the Critical Parent ego state—which generally results in the prospect beating the salesperson down on price, forcing a discount.

Another way the amateur salesperson may react to this situation is to go into a Rebellious Child ego state. While in Rebellious Child, the amateur salesperson enters into a battle with the prospect, which is unlikely to end well for either the prospect or the salesperson. In most cases, the prospect is likely to feel very uncomfortable with being "attacked" by the salesperson.

Prospect: "That's outrageous! I'm not paying that amount of money for your service." (Critical Parent)

Amateur Salesperson: "Don't worry. I'm sure we can get you better pricing—" (Adaptive Child)

Prospect: "Well, you'd better make that happen. Because there's no way I'm going to sign off on a proposal with that kind of pricing." (Critical Parent)

Amateur Salesperson: "Let me go back to the office and speak to my boss. I'm sure we can get you the pricing you are looking for and hopefully get you to sign off by the end of the day." (Adaptive Child)

Gold Medal Salesperson Interaction

The gold medal salesperson realises the prospect is engaging in power-play tactics. With mindfulness, this salesperson does not react to the prospect's Critical Parent ego state and responds instead from a Nurturing Parent ego state. The prospect usually responds in one of two ways: 1) moving into the Nurturing Parent ego state, which is likely to lead to a more constructive outcome (a meeting of equals); or 2) remaining in the Critical Parent ego state, with the most likely outcome of the gold medal salesperson disqualifying the prospect and closing the file.

Prospect: "That's outrageous! I'm not paying that amount of money for your service." (Critical Parent)

Gold Medal Salesperson: "Thank you for sharing that with me. I hope you don't mind, but in all our previous interactions we both agreed that this was the price required in order for us to give you the solution you were looking for. However, if you now feel you don't want to pay that price, I completely understand. And it may be time to remain friends and close the file on this." (Nurturing Parent/Adult)

Prospect: "No, no, no, I do want to go ahead. I was just hoping I might be able to get a better deal—I was probably pushing my luck." (Nurturing Parent/Adult)

Gold Medal Salesperson: "No problem at all. If I were in your position, I might have tried a similar approach. If it's OK with you, shall we now move to signing the contract?" (Nurturing Parent/Adult)

Reflection

People are people, and you are interacting with them all the time. Not only are you interacting with other people, you are also interacting with yourself. It makes sense to have a proven model of human behaviour that you can implement in all your interactions with other people, as well as with yourself. TA is a proven model for understanding human behaviour. With careful study and practice it can optimise all your interactions—and make you a master of the mental game of sales.

SALES MUSCLE #3

Break Out of Bad Patterns

"I want to test my maximum and see how much I can do."

—Michael Phelps

SWIMMER MICHAEL PHELPS, also known as "The Flying Fish," is the most decorated Olympic athlete of all time. His presence in this book, however, has more to do with what happened after he won his astonishing 23 Olympic gold medals than what happened before those triumphs.

This chapter is all about strengthening the muscle that allows you to change your existing habits and move out of your personal comfort zone. Although there were countless times in his athletic career when Phelps had to move beyond what was familiar to him—you don't emerge as the most successful athlete of the Olympics four times in a row without challenging yourself and your own limitations—the thing to notice here has nothing to do with athletic achievement. It has to do with changing your life for the better.

In 2018, two years after his retirement from the world of competitive swimming, Phelps opened up publicly about his personal struggles with attention deficit hyperactivity disorder (ADHD) and depression. He spoke movingly of the many challenges he faced growing up with ADHD and of a particularly dark period after the 2012 Olympics when his depression became so intense that he seriously considered suicide.

Here's the point: Phelps didn't have to go public with that information. He gave up a significant measure of his privacy—which is, make no mistake, a precious commodity for a celebrity of his stature—in sharing what he did with the media. It would have been far simpler and easier, on some level, for him to continue to keep his struggles in these areas private, and I'm sure he was strongly tempted to do just that. He had, after all, been a major star since 2004.

Phelps chose to do what was uncomfortable and unfamiliar to him for the sake of his own personal growth and the growth of others. He realised that he had an opportunity, and even a duty, to help and inspire people facing the same challenges he had faced. He realised that he could make a difference in the lives of others by sharing his own story. Doing so was probably difficult at first, but it ended up allowing him to make a contribution that added new meaning and purpose to his life. That is the way it is with going outside your comfort zones; you only get the reward if you continue to learn and grow, and you only learn and grow by going beyond what is comfortable and familiar.

People are used to talking about Michael Phelps as an Olympic champion, and perhaps as the greatest Olympic champion of all time. That is as it should be. But what they may not realise is that in going outside his comfort zone to be of public service to those struggling with the same daunting challenges he's had to deal with, in being comfortable being uncomfortable, Phelps has shown courage and integrity at a whole new level. In retirement, he's proved himself to be a gold medal performer all over again—by being willing to go consistently outside his comfort zone, because that's where the growth is.

In this chapter, you will learn how you can do the same.

Overcoming the Pattern of Inconsistent Success

Your view of yourself, not the external situation you face, is what keeps you from hitting your targets.

Imagine a journeyman professional men's swimmer (let's call him James) who is ranked 120th in the world for many years.

During the course of the first three years of his career, James is seen as a consistent average performer on the global stage.

Then James begins his eleventh season. He starts to achieve some top 10 finishes and even win some medals. He has a great season—beyond his wildest dreams—and his ranking rises from 120 to 20 in the world standings. He eventually ends the season at #8 in the world. A very strong year!

The next year (his twelfth season), James begins a new round of competition. People in the world of swimming media—and even James himself—are predicting an even greater level of success for James this year.

But James's season collapses. Instead of continuing to progress forward, he starts to place in the bottom half of competitions. At the same time the prior year, he had dominated. But this year, he drops down to 205th on the list of top swimmers. James manages to claw his way back to 118th by the season end, closing out a truly disappointing year that began with such high expectations.

When Your Foot Hurts, You Are Probably Standing on Your Own Toe

James had left his comfort zone with his previous year's success. The following year he subconsciously felt uncomfortable with this newfound success and slowly but surely reverted back to his former bottom-half-of-the-leader-board ways. The result: He slipped back to where he had always been.

The example of James illustrates how easy it is to slip back into one's comfort zone. It does not mean that people cannot change their patterns or that the past defines future behaviour. However, permanent change requires a focused approach towards your mental and emotional state. This requires taking control of empowering beliefs to create the best life possible.

Most people stay in their comfort zones. When you understand the science behind how to break through them, it is easier to move beyond what is familiar and comfortable.

The sales system featured in this book includes a framework called Identity/Role Theory (I/R Theory).* When used correctly, I/R Theory demonstrates how you can break through your comfort zones to attain personal and professional success. Believe it or not, the essence of success is defined more by how you view your success than your external circumstances. This is the formula that Winners know and put into daily practice: "I am responsible for what is in my own head, which in turn determines my performance." At-Leasters and Non-Winners (see below), in contrast, would rather attribute external factors as being responsible for both their successes and their failures.

Here's an example from the world of sales.

A sales coaching client, Emilia, was used to earning an average sales commission of £1,000 per month. She earned this commission for many years. However, one month she closed two very large deals—and achieved a commission of £10,000.

---

* Source: David Sandler

She was overjoyed and, naturally, so was her sales manager. They both expected this stellar performance to continue. Yet the next month, Emilia earned hardly any commission at all.

In the following months Emilia gravitated back to her standard monthly commission of £1,000. Like James in our swimming story, Emilia, the salesperson, achieved great new success levels but could not sustain them. Why? Because she was way out of her current comfort zone.

Both Emilia and James gradually pulled themselves back into their mediocre old comfort zones—which are those of At-Leasters. If Michael Phelps had made the same decision, you would probably never have heard of him.

I/R Theory

I/R Theory can help you break through your comfort zone boundaries and provide a detailed plan to keep breaking through new ones as they arise—to achieve continuous sales improvement, as well as personal and financial freedom.

First, and most important, is your personal identity theory. "I" stands for your identity, or, if you prefer, your self-image, and "R" stands for all the roles you play in your life.

Another way of describing I/R theory is that your "I" side (your identity) is your inner self and your "R" (all the roles you play) is your outer self. This works, too, and it's the version we at Sandler prefer.

Any way you look at it—who you "I" is not what you "R"!

Difference between Your Identity and Role

When you are born, your identity is perfect. On a scale of 1–10, you would say it's an "I"-10. However, as you start growing up, you begin to take on many different roles: student, daughter/son, neighbour, employee, etc. Each person succeeds in some roles and of course, at times, fails in others. For example, you might be picked for the football team and score many goals. Thus, at that time you would rate your role performance as a football player highly with an "R"-9. However, you may also then perform badly on a math test, failing to attain the marks you wanted. Then you may give yourself a role rating of "R"-3 for being a student. As you grow, your identity is formed and initially molded out of your experiences while living these different roles.

Your role ratings can slowly but surely take over your identity, and you can then start to forget about your "I" side. That's a problem. If you forget that you were born an "I"-10, with the corresponding perfect self-image and secure self-esteem, things get mixed up.

Your "I"-10 remains a part of you always and is the foundation of your identity. It's the pure form into which you were born, when you had no roles to play. In truth, you are and always will be an "I"-10—regardless of how you perform in your different roles and activities throughout your life.

In I/R Theory, there are three psychological positions from

which people rate themselves when they let their roles begin to define their identity. Any "I" number less than 10 is short-changing themselves, but people do it anyway.

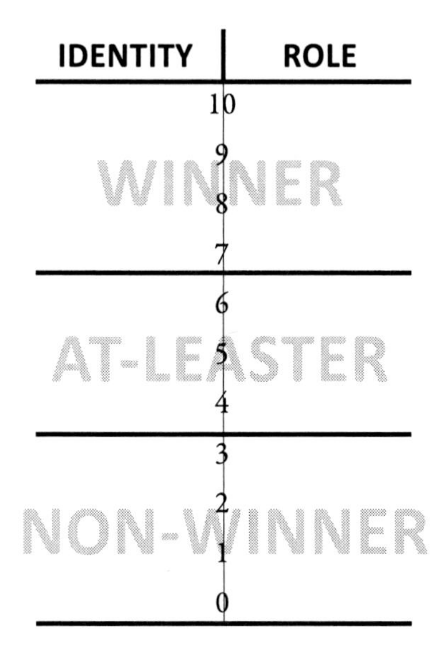

Winners

People who rate their "I" as between 7 and 10 have a very healthy self-image and correspondingly high self-esteem. These Winners feel very good about themselves, irrespective of however they are performing in their roles. They believe they can achieve anything they set their minds to, so they play to win—and expect to achieve. They learn from their mistakes, and they are not afraid to try new things. They also take responsibility for their actions. Most crucial to their success, Winners do not externalise or blame others for their circumstances.

They see themselves as ultimately responsible for what happens, internally and externally.

At-Leasters

At-Leasters (those who rate themselves between 4 and 6) see themselves as average—not so good and not so bad. However, if their performance goes down, the immediate result is that they don't feel good about themselves. Conversely, if they achieve a great result, they then feel elated. At-Leasters rise and fall with the outcome of their actions. They often set modest goals and don't think that they are average—but they are.

Non-Winners

The self-esteem of Non-Winners is totally tied to the result of their performance in their roles, and they don't see themselves as successful in those roles. They rate their "I" as between 0 and 3. As a result, Non-Winners generally associate their endeavors with negative life experiences. These experiences serve to reinforce their guiding assumption that they are not very good at what they try to do and that they will never succeed. Non-Winners don't expect to win, and even when they do, they attribute the win to being lucky. They assume that it could not possibly happen again.

Comfort Zones, by the Numbers

The whole premise of I/R Theory and the science behind breaking through your comfort zones is that if you come to terms with the fact that you will only perform your role in a manner consistent with how you see yourself, then, conceptually, you are halfway out of your comfort zone already. How you feel about yourself (your identity) determines how successful you will be as a person and, in particular, a salesperson. Change how you feel about yourself, and you will change how you feel about going outside what is familiar.

If you see your identity rating as a 6 ("I"-6), then you are an At-Leaster, and you will perform your roles in the 4–6 performance rating range. If you perceive your identity rating as a 9 ("I"-9), then you are a Winner. You will perform your roles in the 7–10 range. Your current comfort zone will always be in the range of one above and one below how you mark your identity rating.

To break out of the comfort zone of being average, it is necessary to separate your identity from the level of your performance in any one role. Unless you work on boosting your identity side, as well as improving your role performance, you will remain in your current comfort zone.

Imagine if, at the dawn of his career, Michael Phelps had never decided to work on boosting his identity and improving his role performance. He might never have won a competition. This is a common trait of high performers in the world of athletics. This principle applies to you, too. On the odd occasion that you outperform your role-performance comfort zone, you then either consciously or subconsciously bring yourself back to your current comfort zone.

The good news is that only you can assign your identity rating—and you are an "I"-10. You always have been an "I"-10 and always will be. It is vitally important to reinforce this belief daily so that it becomes entrenched in your psyche. Once this belief is ingrained, you will have a strong and unflagging self-belief—whatever may transpire externally.

Traditionally in sales, or in any other area of endeavor, people focus on improving their role performance. It can be very difficult to make changes to your role performance. In fact, in order to move towards being a Winner, you will first need to recognise the characteristics of an "I"-10. Second, you will need to recognise what needs to be done to bridge the gap between the current value you have given your "I"-rating (usually considerably lower than 10) and the "I"-10 rating you deserve. Then you must start to believe, in your gut, and consistently, that you are an "I"-10, to build the muscle of self-belief.

It's not a myth. It's not happy talk. It's reality. You really are always a perfect "I"-10, regardless of what is happening in the different roles you play in your life. Learn to recognise this, and then think and act accordingly.

How Winners Think

Below are examples of attributes that make up an "I"-10's list of personality traits. If they are not yet yours, don't worry. By the time you implement the ideas in this book, you will be well on your way to getting there.

"I"-10s:

- Expect to win—so usually do.
- Don't expect winning to be necessarily easy, and understand setbacks are normal.
- Have as their absolute goal to be excellent—never average—in all that they do.
- Have an approach to planning and preparation that is realistic, with incremental "continuous improvement" progress.
- Have guts and determination—they never give up.
- Are willing to try new things and see any flawed attempts as actions from which they can learn.
- Are generous of spirit, which is reflected in their actions.

Joni's Story

Joni worked in a low-level sales support role in an expanding tech company. She had a history of being a hard-working employee, and, even at the relatively low salary of £25,000 per year, she was seen to be highly industrious. The company's sales director, Andrew, was impressed by her diligence and studious approach to her work.

Joni would regularly mention that she would like to buy a house, but on a £25,000 annual salary that simply would not be possible. Andrew saw the inner drive she displayed in her work and felt that within Joni resided a potentially great salesperson in the making. He informed her of the possibility of being promoted from the role of sales support to full-fledged salesperson. If successful, Andrew informed Joni, she could make a lot more money—and be on the road to buying the house of her dreams.

Initially Joni was quite fearful because she had no experience in direct selling. However, Andrew, being trained in the sales system we are sharing with you, was familiar with the programme and its success in developing team members into highly effective salespeople. Andrew also knew, from experience, that great salespeople are not necessarily born, but can be made.

He told Joni that he would put her through the sales training programme and provide her with all the support that she would need. They would work together, he told Joni. In particular, they would focus heavily on the I/R Theory part of the programme. Joni agreed to enroll. With trepidation coupled with excitement of what the future might hold, she transitioned into her new business sales role.

Joni was a better-than-average sales support person, with an "I"-rating of 7 ("I"-7). Together Andrew and Joni co-created a list of "I"-10 attributes that would enable her to become a true Winner salesperson.

Joni's List of "I"-10 Attributes

- I always flourish.

- I have inner calm and confidence.
- I am authentic and stand for my values.
- I am courageous.
- I am strong.
- I am generous.
- I am loving.
- I am highly sought after, just for being me.
- I may get knocked down, but I always get back up.

Joni agreed to look at her "I"-10 list at least five times during her work day. She also took on all the role performance actions required to develop her role performance into an "R"-10. These included Joni building and putting into action her weekly prospecting plan, being accountable for having weekly meetings with Andrew to track and monitor her performance, booking 12 hours of cold calling into her diary weekly, attending two weekly networking events, and committing to ongoing learning and development of Sandler techniques.

After a slow start, Joni's sales performance began to improve dramatically. Within six months of being in her new role she had invoiced a total of £125,000. In addition to her new sales base salary of £40,000, she earned an additional commission of £12,500 in half a year and was on track to earning a total of £65,000 (her base salary plus £25,000 in sales commissions)—almost three times what she earned in her former sales support role.

Joni attributed her amazing superstar success to the breaking of her patterns and comfort zones. Of course, she continued to improve her performance according to a range of factors, but the most important one was her change of attitude. In particular, her current conviction and unshakeable self-belief that if she works hard every day to keep maintaining and believing that she has an identity rating of 10 ("I"-10), she cannot help but achieve her goals—with a corresponding Winner role performance of 10 ("R"-10).

LIZ'S STORY

Liz, a business owner, had been working very hard for five years. She felt she had reached a stage where she had everything in place to take her business to the next level for a massive revenue increase. She then decided to share her plans with a very close, respected business advisor. When she told this advisor that she was going to increase sales by 400% in the following year, the advisor told Liz that he did not think that this increase was possible. Instead the advisor suggested that Liz aim for a 200% increase. Liz, however, maintained her belief that it was possible to generate a 400% increase due to all the hard work and planning she had put into the past five years. Liz backed up this belief by putting into practice her new sales plans.

In Q1 of the following year, Liz did achieve a 400% increase over the previous year's quarter. She was surprised as much as overjoyed. Her "I"-rating was 7, so the 400% increase was an "R"-10 rating, which was out of her current comfort zone.

Unsurprisingly, Liz's Q2 slumped back to the level her advisor had predicted. However, this slump motivated Liz to review the I/R Theory concepts very carefully. She studied the concepts until she really understood that in order to maintain an overall high role performance, she had to start believing that she was an "I"-10. Liz also now understood that her role performance would correspond to either 1 point above or 1 point below her "I"-rating.

Liz's next step was to rewrite her list of what an "I"-10 looked like and to review that "I"-10 list every day. Within a short time, she started to deeply believe that she was an "I"-10. Her role performance stayed at a high level for the remainder of the year, and for Q3 and Q4 she again achieved her 400% sales increase.

Liz had learned how to put I/R Theory into practice, and her sales success was testimony to the effective implementation of this theory.

REFLECTION

Most salespeople are in a comfort zone, whether conscious or subconscious. It is very hard to become a successful salesperson if you are not willing to move out of your comfort zone. Fortunately, there is a science that enables people to break out of their comfort zones—I/R Theory. Application of this I/R Theory on the surface appears relatively simple and straightforward. However, in practice it requires mindfulness and a willingness to push through homeostasis and break the underlying "fear of success" head-trash paradigm. Like Michael Phelps, we each have the potential to break through what is familiar to us, and to move consistently to new levels of personal growth, achievement, and contribution.

SALES MUSCLE #4

Decide What You Want and Build a Plan

"Disappointment and adversity can be catalysts for greatness. There's something particularly exciting about being the hunter, as opposed to the hunted. And that can make for powerful energy."

—CATHY FREEMAN

SPRINTER CATHY FREEMAN was the first Australian Indigenous person to become a Commonwealth Games gold medalist. She did so at the tender age of 16 in 1990. Her breakthrough season came four years later, when she won solo gold in both the 200 metre and 400 metre events at the Commonwealth Games, and competed as a member of Australia's 4 × 100 metre squad, winning the silver medal. During that

1994 season, when Freeman emerged as one of the world's elite competitors in track and field, she shaved 1.3 seconds off her personal best in the 400 meter event, and also set personal bests in the 100 meter and 200 meter events.

The stage was set for a high-profile performance at the 1996 Olympics at Atlanta, and Freeman did not disappoint. In a 400-meter medal race that is now considered one of the greatest of all time, Freeman battled her French rival Marie-José Pérec down the stretch, but found herself outkicked in the final seconds. Freeman had to settle for a silver medal, but the world had been put on notice that Freeman was making a claim for the title of greatest female sprinter on earth, and that she had her eyes set on Olympic gold.

And then, in 1997, Freeman suffered a major setback. She seriously injured her foot in a race in Oslo. She missed the entire 1998 season.

Notice: Freeman sat out that entire season on purpose. It was part of her long-term plan to be in peak condition in time for the 2000 Olympics, which, as fate would have it, were to be held in her home country. Freeman had a clear goal—a first-place finish at the Sydney Olympics—and she knew, as all elite athletes know, that such objectives do not attain themselves. She took nothing for granted. She and her coaches set up a long-term plan for recovery, she examined that plan from every possible angle, and she followed it to the letter, devoting an entire athletic season to its fulfillment.

The result was a triumph in Sydney: Freeman lit the Olympic flame, outperformed her rival Pérec (who failed to make the finals), won the 400-meter gold medal, and claimed her place as a national hero in Australia. Quite an accomplishment for someone who, as a young runner, routinely won school races—and saw the medals and trophies that were rightfully hers handed over to white competitors. Of her role in Australia's checkered history on racial matters, Freeman had this to say: "I have been told many times that when I win I make my people proud to be Australian. I am Aboriginal, I am one of them, and every time I win or am honoured like this, it should be an example to Aboriginal people who may think they have nowhere to go but down. But more importantly, I am an Australian and I would like to make all Australians feel proud to be Australian. Ours is a truly multicultural society and should be united as such. I would like to believe that my successes are celebrated by all Australians, bringing our nation together."

With her victory in the 2000 Olympics, Freeman emerged, not only as a hero for Indigenous peoples and for Australians, but as a hero for all people. That victory would not have been possible without Freeman's capacity to set up a plan for success, and her willingness to work that plan in a disciplined way, following a major injury.

Just like Freeman, professional salespeople must have a plan for success—a prospecting plan.

Gold Medal Salespeople Have a Prospecting Plan

Most salespeople do not enjoy prospecting. In fact, when it comes to prospecting, the majority of salespeople would rather be doing almost anything else. It's fair to say that the act of contacting someone you have never met with the aim of eventually asking for money does not come naturally to most people. It can make people feel uncomfortable, nervous, and even fearful.

But what is the result of never prospecting or reaching out to potential buyers? Lackluster or even non-existent sales.

In a perfect world, people would actively seek you out, begging to buy from you. Of course, with savvy marketing techniques, intuitive websites, and excellent commercial e-platforms, you can generate incoming leads to contact. Still, no matter how great the return of such methods, salespeople know that they will eventually need to reach out to strangers with the goal of selling to them. This is what it means to be a salesperson.

The Amateur Salesperson's Approach to Prospecting

Amateur salespeople come up with lots of creative ways to avoid prospecting activities. They may prefer writing proposals and creating intricate reports or attending meetings for a good catch up with people they already know (but whom they know will never buy). Or, they may spend time crafting clever but unproductive email campaigns, fussing over each word and the syntactical structure of the message. They do anything but actually reach out to someone one-on-one.

These are the tactics of amateur salespeople. They would rather stay in the comfort zone of frivolous activities than boldly build business for themselves and their company. The outcome of this delayed prospecting approach—or plain avoidance!—is mediocre sales results, lower commissions, and less money earned. When cold calling or direct prospecting does occur, amateur salespeople want to be off the phone as fast as possible. There usually isn't a plan in place, and if there is, it is not followed.

Wearing Two Hats

Samuel, a small business owner, can't afford to hire a salesperson. So, in addition to running his business, he has to wear the sales hat, too.

He does ad hoc prospecting—when he has the time. With no proper plan, his success is erratic. He is often very stressed and locked into a feast-or-famine business model.

Samuel is surviving, but he often has cash flow issues, which increase his stress levels. His sales results are inconsistent—ad hoc prospecting does not generate consistent results—which keeps Samuel up at night.

Gold Medal Salespeople's Approach to Prospecting

So how do gold medal salespeople approach their prospecting activities?

They are focused and diligent with their prospecting calls. They may not enjoy prospecting or look forward to it; however, they know that every prospecting call is an opportunity to earn money by making a sale.

Gold medal salespeople know that the purpose of prospecting is to initiate the sales process, create bonding and rapport, and establish a positive and professional relationship with the person they are contacting. They know what they are striving to achieve. They know that there will be many more *noes* than *yesses* in their sales activities; however, they see setbacks as a natural part of the overall selling process.

You can compare the importance of having a methodical, disciplined sales plan with the dedicated methods of training that Olympic athletes use—including their physical workout regime, diet plan, and even how they relax and when they go to bed. This is all done with the goal of achieving the results for which they are striving.

Remember: It's of no value at all to have a plan and not stick to it. Consistency is vital.

CREATING YOUR TAILORED PLAN FOR SALES SUCCESS

People create financial goals for themselves because achieving them allows greater freedom to make the best choices possible for their lives. The way to accomplish this is to have a plan. First, establish your sales goals. Then, build a structured plan to achieve them.

Let's write down a step-by-step plan for how you can achieve your sales goals as a gold medal salesperson. Each market is different, and many people have different goals that they are working toward. What matters is that you have a practical plan that you write down to help make your sales ambitions a reality.

1. **Step 1:** Think about how much money you would like to earn in the year and write this down.
2. **Step 2:** Divide this figure by 12 to identify how much you need to earn per month. This is important, as it breaks the number down into workable chunks to be dealt with monthly. Also, it can reveal whether the number is realistic.
3. **Step 3:** Now calculate how much you need to sell to hit this sales target.

Build this projection into your quarterly, monthly, and weekly prospecting plans, with the required mix and quantity of prospecting activities that lead to revenue. For example, determine the number of calls you need to make each day, how many networking events you need to attend, and the amount of time you spend on social selling platforms and digital marketing, such as LinkedIn, your email campaigns, and efforts to forge strategic alliances, in order to sell at that level.

Jasmine Hits Her Target Via Her Structured Sales Plan

Jasmine, a salesperson whose primary prospecting activity is cold calling, has a goal to generate one sale worth £10,000 every week.

In order to achieve her goal, she follows the process below:

- Jasmine has noticed over her career that if she gets four new prospects per week to agree to schedule a 15-minute exploratory call, she will most likely close one sale per week.
- She also knows that out of every two people who take her initial cold call, one of them will agree to schedule a 15-minute exploratory call. So, she needs eight calls in which she gets through to a person to get four scheduled for the 15-minute call.
- She knows that in general, about 10% of the calls she makes will get through to an actual person (most people won't take her call or are out of the office). So, to get eight calls with a person, she'll need to make 80 calls per week.

- In short: 80 calls per week leads to eight calls with a person, which leads to four 15-minute exploratory calls, which leads to one sale.

Jasmine is a professional salesperson. She knows that by diligently making 80 cold calls consistently and effectively every week, she will hit her target of one sale of £10,000 a week. She is following a systematic sales process. Jasmine is confident and relaxed (and relatively stress free) since she knows that she is likely to almost always hit—or exceed—her weekly sales targets.

Control Your Destiny with a Weekly Prospecting Plan

Tom is a software salesperson. In order to hit his annual sales numbers, he needs to have a weekly prospecting plan with a mix of different prospecting activities. Sandler's Cookbook for Success is a tool that assembles different ingredients in the appropriate quantities, just like a recipe in a cookbook.

Tom's weekly Cookbook for Success:

1. 40 cold calls per day (10 hours a week)
2. 1 hour of research per day (5 hours a week)
3. 1 hour on LinkedIn per day (5 hours a week)
4. 2 networking events per week (6 hours a week)
5. 1 hour of follow-up calls per day (5 hours a week)
6. 2 client meetings per week (4 hours a week)
7. 45–50 minutes of writing proposals (4 hours a week)

Track Your Progress and Fine-Tune Your Plan

The gold medal salesperson has a prospecting plan that is acted upon, measured, and aligned with the sales goals set to achieve in the year ahead. This plan should be monitored and reviewed to assess where the best results are coming from and where the weaknesses lie.

It is vital to monitor the activities that have been set out in your plan, such as tracking how many times you dial per day to cold call, how many events you attend, and how many leads you discover with the aim of doing business.

From there you can tailor your plan and fine-tune it to calibrate it effectively to yield the best sales results possible. Amateur salespeople may have a plan, but under stress, they often abandon it. Gold medal salespeople know that the route to success isn't easy, but the plan to achieve it must be followed to attain what is desired.

Reflection

Most salespeople may have a plan for achieving their sales goals, but that plan might be only ad hoc at best. The consequences of an ad hoc plan are inconsistent actions, which result in inconsistent sales results. Gold medal salespeople have very focused sales goals and build a systematic plan with consistent and focused actions, which means they generally achieve consistent sales results.

SALES MUSCLE #5

Take Responsibility for Motivating Yourself

"When I began to realise I was pretty good at rowing, my ambition was an Olympic gold medal. Simple as that. One gold medal was my goal. I achieved that in Los Angeles, ahead of schedule. Why didn't I stop then? The answer is simple: I thought I could do better and win another one."

—STEVE REDGRAVE

STEVE REDGRAVE—also known as Sir Steven Geoffrey Redgrave, CBE, DL—is widely regarded as the greatest British Olympian. As a rower, Redgrave won gold medals at five consecutive Olympic Games. No. That is not a misprint. He really did win gold for Great Britain in 1984, 1988, 1992, 1996, and 2000. Redgrave is the only man to win gold medals at five different Olympic Games in an endurance sport, meaning a sport that tests physical strength and resilience under pressure. Redgrave has also won three Commonwealth Games gold medals and nine World Rowing Championships golds. He is the most successful male rower in Olympic history. That kind of achievement is impossible without strong personal motivation, which is what this chapter is all about.

When asked to identify the critical factor in his success as a rower, Redgrave had this to say: "Self-belief is probably the most crucial factor in sporting success. The bodies are roughly equal, the training is similar, the techniques can be copied. What separates the achievers is nothing as tangible as split times or kilograms. It's the iron in the mind, not in the supplements, that wins medals."

The "iron in the mind" Redgrave is referring to can be thought of as the personal will to be the best you can be—that driving internal desire to make the most you possibly can of your capacities, your opportunities, and your resources. This self-renewing personal resolve is why Redgrave didn't stop at one gold medal. It's a consistent trait of gold medal athletes like Redgrave, and it is also a consistent trait of gold medal salespeople. They motivate themselves.

It is worth noting here that, having finally retired from athletics, Redgrave has sought out new goals and challenges. He is now an author and a sought-after motivational speaker, and he's helping others to build up the "iron in the mind" that led him to such amazing levels of achievement as a rower. Redgrave is currently earning great reviews on the speaking circuit. No surprise there. He's highly motivated!

Amateurs Don't Have Smart Goals

Amateur athletes generally do not train rigorously. They will not compete if they don't feel like doing so. Sometimes there are not enough players on the teams, so they borrow players. There is little preparation in both a physical and mental sense.

Most amateur athletes are motivated by having fun. The desire to win or lose can fluctuate. In an amateur rugby team, the players may even go out and party the night before a game. Typically, amateur athletes are not goal-driven. Therefore, their motivation is inconsistent and does not drive them towards excellent performance.

Similarly, the motivation of an amateur salesperson ebbs and flows. One day it is high and they can take on the world, and the next day they are asking, "Why in the world did I go into sales?" They rely for motivation on their sales manager, who generally provides carrot-and-stick strategies.

These strategies are destined to generate mediocre sales performance at best. The challenge with carrot-and-stick motivation is that there are a finite number of carrots that can be used to motivate activity. Eventually amateur salespeople put down the tools, become complacent with the amount of carrots they have, and are not personally driven to achieve consistent sales performance.

Amateur salespeople also develop a tolerance to the pain. This includes threats of firing from the manager above them, no (or little) commission month after month, and no real consequences for non-performance. They become complacent if the sticks or carrots are not used effectively. If the threats or promises that are made are not followed through, the sales results continue to limp along with an average bottom line.

The Gold Medal Approach to Motivation

Gold medal salespeople, however, are connected to their own personal goals and what they want to achieve. The system in this book enables salespeople to maintain effective and consistent motivation at all times. The alignment of personal goals is linked to sales targets and desired growth.

As was said in an earlier chapter, most people do not believe that dreams can become a reality and they are stuck in their comfort zone. Successful people know their dreams deserve to become their reality. Believing you deserve your deepest goals is vitally important to motivating yourself to bring what you want to fruition.

To Achieve Bold Goals, Connect with Your Deepest Ambitions

The emphasis in this chapter is on staying motivated and connected to your goals—day after day after day. However, when it comes to connecting to your deepest dreams and goals, it is not always easy to work this out by yourself. You may be stuck in a comfort zone or in a pattern of behaviour you are not able to break.

Some reasons many people are not personally connected and committed to their life goals:

- They may not have a clear purpose in their life. Most people fit this category, and this is no judgment on those who do not have such a purpose. However, having a clear purpose tends to translate into having life goals and actions that lead to success.
- They may suffer from a lack of confidence so therefore they do not set many goals. Moreover, even when they set them, they are usually modest goals. This lack of confidence translates into weak ambition and drive.
- They may have been burned when they set goals in the past when they did not achieve them. Instead of seeing this experience as a lesson learned, people in this category are resistant to setting goals now since they fear the same feelings they had when they failed before.
- They might not actually know how to set goals, i.e., they don't have a systematic process. They may be aware that there are goal-setting processes they could investigate, but might be skeptical that any of these processes would ever work for them personally.

Procrastination and Other Excuses

Some people have goals and clearly defined actions, but procrastinate when the time comes to take action. This could involve feeling that they have more important things to do and making a decision to do those important things with the intention to take action on their goals later. (That action, however, seldom happens.) Or, they find it very difficult to get started at all.

Others might habitually blame their lack of action on other people or things. This is often displayed in spending a lot of time making excuses and then possibly sharing these excuses with as many people as possible. This is called externalising. For some, this becomes a deeply ingrained behaviour pattern that is very hard to break. Externalising leaves little time for taking the appropriate actions required to achieve goals.

Some people may also spend a lot of time living in the past or in the future. They might be trying to re-create a past when they had felt happy or fantasising about a fabulous future. Both lead to taking little action to improve today.

Then there are people who are inefficient with actions they take because they have no systematic process. This might be due to lack of planning or merely a long-held pattern of working inefficiently. Regardless of whether this inefficiency is subconscious or conscious, the pattern is often very difficult to break.

Change Is Hard

Change is critical to developing, growing, and attaining goals. However, change is not necessarily easy. In many cases, it is extremely difficult. Change also means moving through one's comfort zones. While comfort zones might have their own drawbacks and people might be bored and frustrated by them, when push comes to shove and action is required to move out of them, most people choose the easy option to remain—not changing at all.

Change means giving up old habits and patterns of behaviour. These old habits can die hard. Change also involves becoming an adult and giving up on acting out and behaving like a child. This is clearly logical, but again, putting this into practice is often too difficult.

It's a fact that change and transformation require one to keep going, even when it gets very tough. Many people actually give up even when the end goal may be close to being achieved.

Dedication and commitment to change requires trusting that by having a plan and taking the relevant actions, the result becomes more and more probable. The challenge is that this requires a strong self-belief and optimism, and this can often be lacking. Let's look at why this is so.

Fight the Monster of Homeostasis

The theory of homeostasis may help clarify why it is so difficult to make behavioural change. Homeostasis is a physiological, self-regulatory process within the human body—an automatic built-in response that always maintains a normal body temperature. When the human body goes below a particular low temperature, it automatically starts shivering to get back to normal. When it gets too hot, it will sweat for the same reason.

The theory of homeostasis is a powerful metaphor for what happens when people try to make a change. There is a physiological function that will kick in whenever you try to change that will work to keep you exactly where you are already. Homeostasis is a monster that does not want you to change any aspect of your life. It needs to be fought each and every day if you are to implement the actions to achieve your goals.

Whenever you feel resistance to doing what is needed to achieve your goals, it is most likely homeostasis in action.

Build the Homeostasis-Defeating Muscle

When you experience the resistance that is homeostasis, you need to plow on, taking the actions you have committed to take to achieve your goals. The more you put this into practice, the stronger your homeostasis-defeating muscle becomes.

However, in order to build the fire of internal motivation, you also need a powerful, deep, personal, and emotional connection to your dreams and life goals. One way of doing this is to create a dream board, which is a transformational tool for creating and supporting this kind of personal commitment.

A dream board is a visual tool used to clarify, concentrate, and maintain focus on specific life goals. It is a visual representation of your dreams and your ideal life.

Dare to dream what you really want for your life. Don't limit yourself by wondering what you will need to do in order to manifest your dreams—just dream.

Focusing on what you desire, not how you are going to go about it, is key to a successful dream board. The *how* will be dealt with later when you formulate an action plan to achieve your goals. Once you conceive your aspirations deeply and connect them very closely to what you desire, you can then work to develop the *how*.

Start the Process of Building a Dream Board

Try to visualise, if you can, the age when you might leave this planet. Visualise yourself at that age looking back over your life and asking yourself: "What do I want to achieve and have in my life by the time I depart this world?"

Then go to an online search-engine to pick five to eight images that correspond to those visualisations. Spend at least an hour doing this exercise. Make sure that each image you pick resonates with you. Copy these images into a document or print them out, and arrange them in a way that is aesthetically pleasing to you. Voila! You have created your first dream board.

Create three laminated dream boards—one that you keep next to your computer or in your office, one that you put in your briefcase or bag, and one that you put in your home (often the best place is on the fridge). Look at that dream board throughout the day. Over time, with your dreams at the forefront of your thoughts, you will discover ways to manifest them.

Andrea's Dream House

Andrea was initially quite skeptical of the concept of dream boards. However, after some encouragement, she reluctantly agreed to build her first one.

She then put down eight images of what she dreamed to have in her life in a document as described above, and followed the instructions of looking at her dream board regularly.

Six months later she showed up for a coaching session and explained that she had moved into a new apartment on the river. She also shared with us that when she sat at her dream board, she saw that the flat she had moved into was right next door to the flat she had placed a photograph of on her dream board. Amazing!

Suffice to say, Andrea is now a great fan of dream board and accepts (as we do) that they work powerfully but mysteriously, harnessing forces that operate somehow at a subliminal level when you look at the dream board every day. Every year Andrea creates a new dream board. It's a good idea to do what she does and take the dream board process very seriously.

Farhad's Dreams for His Daughter

Farhad had been running a small technology company for many years. When he came for sales training, his company was stuck in a comfort zone, with revenues and profits that had been plateauing for several years.

As part of his training, Farhad created a dream board that was filled with "feeling" dream images, connected to his young daughter's needs. He dreamed of moving to a larger house for her and having enough money to send her to a private school. However, with his company stagnating, he did not have the money.

Farhad looked at his dream board over a six-month period. Eventually, a new level of motivation emerged in him. He started to take actions to drive his business to the next level—something he had not done for many years.

Over a three-year period, Farhad doubled the profitability of his company by taking bold action he would not have taken before. This new growth provided him with the money to achieve his dreams for his daughter. Farhad now swears by the powerful nature of building dream boards that are deeply connected to one's aspirations and goals.

So—what goals should you build your dream board around?

It is often very helpful to have an experienced coach who has been through this process and can be both supportive and give tough love when required. A Sandler coach is trained in understanding the importance of being deeply connected and committed to your personal dreams and goals as a way of motivating yourself to take all the actions required to achieve greatness—whether that be in the area of sales or in one's personal life.

A 10-Step Systematic Approach for Goal Setting

Goals should be SMART, defined as specific, measurable, attainable, realistic, and time-driven. They should always be written down. They should cover both the short term and long term, and if possible, they should cover all areas of one's life so that the total goal package is holistic and all-encompassing.

There are eight types of goals:

- Social
- Physical
- Spiritual
- Mental
- Work (Career)
- Family
- Personal
- Financial

Set Your Goals

Once again, imagine the year that you will be departing this planet (not that anyone knows the exact date for certain). Write down that year, whatever it is, and then fast-forward to that time.

This exercise can be done alone, but often it is productive to do it with other people—family, friends, or anyone who plays a supportive role in your life. Allow yourself at least four hours to complete this 10-step systematic process for goal setting.

STEP 1

- Gather eight pieces of paper and label each page with one of the eight life goal areas.
- On each page write a brief summary of where you currently are in relation to this life goal area.

STEP 2

- Place a circle in the middle of each page and draw lines that point outwards from the circle. Then allow yourself to feel what you would like to accomplish in the future. Write these goals on the lines.

STEP 3

- For each piece of paper with a different life goal area, prioritise and pick the three most important goals.

STEP 4

- On a new piece of paper, create a master list of the top three goals in all of the eight areas.

STEP 5

- Check for any conflicts. If you can, try to make sure the goals are not too heavily weighted in one or two areas. The more holistic your goals are, the more likely you are to achieve them.

STEP 6

- Write a detailed description of how you are going to achieve these goals. This is your action plan. It's important to decide what you are going to do now and what you are going to do in the future. Take care not to overload yourself with too many actions in the present. However, it is good to stretch yourself by having bold and audacious goals.

STEP 7

- Breaking down the goals and actions into short-term goals and actions can be a very powerful way of building the goal-setting and attainment "muscle." Three months (12 weeks) can be a very effective time frame for establishing a life-long pattern of generating and sustaining the fire of internal motivation.

STEP 8

- Share your goals with others, especially those who will be impacted by the goals: friends, family, colleagues, or people you like and respect and who like and respect you. This creates a powerful statement of intent from yourself that you are deeply committed and connected to your goals.

STEP 9

- Review your goals and try to fine-tune them on a weekly basis. Obtaining valued accountability from others provides support and encouragement, as well as objective sanity checks.

STEP 10

- Be courageous, tenacious, and persistent. Goal setting can be challenging since it pushes you through your comfort zones. Remember that it is important to keep going, even when the going gets tough. The ROI of goal setting will reward the effort and courage of sticking to the process.

Reflection

Sales success is often more about perspiration than inspiration. A salesperson's week is often full of activities (some of them tedious, and others downright dull), and there will be many highs and lows. The gold medal salesperson understands that a high level of motivation is required to sustain consistently high performance. This person understands that optimum motivation is maintained by having a strong emotional connection to their goals.

SALES MUSCLE #6

Take Control of the Process

"They all fall in the round I call."

—Muhammad Ali

MUHAMMAD ALI'S IMPACT has been felt the world over, in and out of the boxing ring. His story began in Louisville, Kentucky, a deeply segregated town in the southern United States. Gifted with physical talents and an innate self-belief that he had the ultimate control of himself and his destiny, Ali pulled himself out of poverty, struggle, and injustice to become a three-time heavyweight champion of the world, acclaimed civil rights icon, global humanitarian—and arguably "the greatest of all time." In 1960, Ali won the Olympic gold medal in light heavyweight boxing. Prior and post-victory, he proclaimed, "I am the king," displaying a confidence and a willingness to influence the public narrative about him that would define his entire career.

In the boxing ring, Ali's desire to control his opponents was legendary. Before a fight, he would even predict the round and manner in which he would defeat an opponent. In 1964, Ali dealt Sonny Liston a devastating defeat and colossal upset win at odds of 7 to 1, with 43 out of 46 sports writers stating that he would lose. Ali went on to win. In the rematch, Ali called him out and said that he would conquer him in the first round—which he did. Archie Moore and Henry Copper also fell at the pre-appointed time, called by the Nostradamus of professional men's boxing.

Ali was also able to take charge when almost no one gave him a chance. In 1974, a much older Ali faced undefeated world heavyweight champion George Foreman in the historic "Rumble in the Jungle" boxing event in Kinshasa, Zaire. Ali won by knockout, putting Foreman down just before the end of the eighth round. Ali returned to the ring and won the World Title belt a further two times, to end his career with a 56-5 win/lose ratio. Most uniquely, Ali is the only boxer in history to have won the Heavyweight World Championship three times in his career.

It takes incredible strength and character to stand up for what you believe in and live or die according to your word. Ali had that strength. On April 28, 1967, Ali refused induction into the U.S. Army as he was unwilling to take up arms against the people of Vietnam, whom he felt had done nothing to him to warrant an action as drastic as war. He claimed conscientious objector status due to religious beliefs (he had become a Muslim in the early 1960s) and was stripped of his World Championship title. He was convicted for draft evasion and was forbidden to box professionally (at the time he was at the peak of his career). Ali appealed the case to the U.S. Supreme Court and won, but he lost three and a half precious years during his physical prime due to sanctions that had been placed on him by U.S. boxing authorities.

In 1971, he began a comeback that established him as one of the greatest athletes of the twentieth century. This phase of his career included several historic boxing matches and feuds, notably fights with Joe Frazier and George Foreman. The most important bout with Foreman, mentioned above, has been called "arguably the greatest sporting event of the twentieth century." Ali defeated the younger, stronger, and faster Foreman by exhausting him, taking on the role of a human punching bag in the early rounds and then seizing control of the fight in the eighth round with a flurry of devastating punches that led the referee to declare a technical knockout.

Win or lose, Ali's was the unbound voice, defending what he believed to be right, even when his life, his reputation, and liberty were at stake. He became an important and influential spokesman for African Americans, for Muslims, and for young people in the tumultuous period of the late 1960s and early 1970s, and he was also a powerful role model for the disabled in the physically challenging later years of his life.

It has been estimated that he took over 200,000 hits during the course of his boxing career. In 1996, suffering from Parkinson's disease, Ali lit the flame at the 1996 Summer Olympics in Atlanta, Georgia, a remarkable moment shared by an estimated 3.5 billion viewers worldwide. In 2012, although frail, he bore the Olympic flag during the opening ceremonies of the 2012 Summer Olympics in London. He died in 2016.

On Athletes and the Rules They Follow

Muhammad Ali was at his greatest when he took control. Like the great athlete he was, he knew the rules and followed them, but purposefully, and to his strategic advantage. To give just one example: Ali never violated the rules of the boxing ring during the "Rumble in the Jungle" match, but cannily used those rules to his advantage in creating a series of opportunities for Foreman to punch himself into a state of exhaustion. Ali worked the rulebook, and in so doing he executed a clear plan. He didn't let his opponent work him.

It's worthwhile at this point to step back and discuss the whole concept of rules. In casual sporting events, there are, theoretically, a set of rules that govern the game. However, these rules are not always strictly followed. Think of playing a game of football with your mates. There usually isn't a referee, and if there is, it may be an injured friend who knows the game well enough but may make highly questionable and inconsistent calls. Little respect is given to such a referee, and the players sometimes hurl abuse at the source of those questionable calls, who may even have a beer in their hand. But it is all in fun. After all, these are amateur players.

Now let's look at Olympic athletes. In rugby sevens, for instance (which is indeed an Olympic sport), the referee commands the utmost respect from the participants, just as they do in the sport of boxing. In fact, in rugby, the referee is generally just as fit as the players are! Rugby referees are trained and participate in courses and workshops to keep abreast of new rules and regulations as they come into effect. If they start slipping in their performance, they can be called before a tribunal to be assessed and can be fined, demoted to lower divisions, or fired altogether. Professional rugby pitches are immaculate, with lines clearly outlined. With the advent of television, official calls that are questionable are referred to the camera and reviewed so that (most of the time) the correct calls are made. The ground rules for rugby are strictly laid out and consistently adhered to, just as they are in a major boxing match. The point here is that gold medal players who know the rules use that knowledge strategically as they carry out their plan for the match, just as Ali did during his legendary bout with Foreman.

Amateur Salespeople Let the Prospect Control the Sales Process

Now that you know how important rules and referees/umpires are for gold medal athletes, let's take a look at amateur salespeople and the guidelines they subconsciously establish with their prospects. Amateur salespeople mistakenly assume that there is mutual understanding between themselves and their prospects in regard to how the sales procedures will be conducted.

Jim is a sole proprietor accountant. He does no prospecting so he is generally very subservient in any sales interaction. When Jim attends a sales meeting, the prospect quickly takes control of the meeting and cuts short any questioning Jim may attempt. The prospect pressures Jim into presenting his solution, and this generally results in the prospect taking charge of the next steps. The next steps usually involve the prospect saying something along the lines of, "Send me a proposal, and I will get back to you."

The above meeting scenario is Jim's standard approach and the reason for his truly lackluster conversion rate to date.

Gold Medal Salespeople Take Control with an Up-Front Contract

On the other hand, as it is in professional sports, a sales situation often begins as a contest between two parties: the buyer and the seller. Both parties have an objective that they are seeking to achieve. However, often the rules governing their behaviour are not clear to each other. The Up-Front Contract (see more details in Chapter 8) fixes this problem by demonstrating, once and for all, how salespeople can get prospects to play by the rules and (eventually) to disclose the truth.

Gold medal salespeople understand that there needs to be a meeting of equals with whomever they are interacting. This holds true whether prospects are associates or CEOs. Gold medal salespeople value their own time and energy and do not waste it on prospects who will never buy or want to take advantage of valuable resources. By creating the environment of a meeting of equals, gold medal salespeople maintain their self-esteem and confidence.

Gold medal salespeople don't let themselves get pushed into pitching. They make sure that each step of the sales process is conducted with clarity and mutual agreement. There is no "mutual mystification" (confusion between the salesperson and the prospect about what the agenda is).

How is this done? It is achieved by establishing up-front contracts with the prospect at the beginning and end of each interaction and sales meeting. Furthermore, mini up-front contracts are established and used throughout the sales conversations to ensure clarity every step of the way.

Five Elements of the Up-Front Contract

The up-front contract consists of five elements.

1. Establish the purpose of the interaction (i.e., the meeting or phone call).

- This is important because often there is a lack of clarity between the buyer and the seller as to what the goal of the conversation is.

2. Determine the length of the interaction.

- Sometimes a salesperson will make an assumption that the time parameters of a call or meeting have been agreed upon. However, this is often not the case at all. Not doing so puts the buyer in control of the sales interaction.
- With no time rule, the buyer could, at any time during the meeting, say something like, "Time is running out. I have a meeting to get to. Show me what you can offer." This can lead to a premature presentation, with the seller buckling under pressure to disclose the features and benefits of the product or service before feeling ready.
- To avoid such a pressure scenario, it is vital for the salesperson to get mutual agreement on the length of time of the meeting or sales call.

3. Explore the prospect's agenda and expectations.

- It is important to discover at the beginning of the meeting exactly what the prospect would like to achieve by the end of the meeting.

- This is a very powerful tactic, as it forces the buyer to tell the salesperson what the expectation is by meeting end—giving insight as to what must be dealt with by the salesperson in the course of the interaction.
- It is also extremely useful since if the buyer does not want to share this information, it is often a sign that the salesperson is spending time with an information gatherer or time waster. True prospects are generally more than happy to share what they are looking to have as a desirable outcome for the meeting.

4. Share the salesperson's agenda and expectations.

- Here the salesperson sets the agenda by letting the prospect know that the salesperson is going to ask questions first. This ensures the salesperson qualifies the prospect deeply before presenting any solutions.
- This avoids the scenario of the salesperson agreeing to write lengthy proposals for clients who will never buy. Another key part of the gold medal salesperson's agenda is to let the prospect know that doing business with the prospect may not be right for the salesperson. In this case, the salesperson would say something along the lines of: "There may not be a good fit here, and if this is the case we can part as friends." This differentiates the gold medal salesperson from the amateur, since

there are no false promises and an equal business stature is maintained.

5. ***Identify mutually-agreed-upon next steps.***

- Amateur salespeople generally talk about next steps at the end of the meeting. This tends to give the buyer control. (As in the above example with Jim, the buyer asked him to "send a proposal.") By agreeing together about the steps at the end of the meeting, there will be defined expectations for going forward.

NOTE: The gold medal salesperson has only three potential next steps:

1. Giving the prospect the opportunity to say no. The buyer then has the chance to tell the truth, and the salesperson wastes no time and energy chasing a slow *no* or non-opportunity.
2. Giving the salesperson the potential to say no. This keeps the balance of power with the salesperson and encourages the salesperson to be seen as a professional who is not desperate.
3. Letting the prospect know that if there is a good fit, the salesperson and the prospect can both come together to create mutually-agreed-upon next steps together. Wishy-washy words like, "I'd like to think it over," are unacceptable to the gold medal salesperson.

Establishing an up-front contract at the beginning and end of each sales call, meeting, and presentation calls for guts and the willingness to push through one's comfort zones. To set up-front contracts that hold yourself and the other people accountable is the strongest possible strategy to achieve success and to maximise the efficiency of your valuable time.

A Gold Medal Salesperson Controls the Sales Process

Now let's look at practical applications of the up-front contract, as used by gold medal salesperson Linda.

Like Jim, Linda is a sole proprietor accountant. However, Linda is also a trained sales professional. Thus, Linda sets up-front contracts in all her sales and prospecting interactions. Here's an example of Linda at work.

"Hi there, I am Linda from ABC Accounting. Thank you very much for inviting me in today to talk about your accounting challenges." This opening is very different from the normal introduction between amateur salespeople and prospects. The usual result is inconsequential chitchat, which leads to the prospect taking control of the meeting and initiating an imbalanced relationship between the prospect and the salesperson going forward. Linda's professional opening, on the other hand, creates equal business stature between the parties and sets the correct tone of mutual respect.

Linda then says: "I know we have an hour in the schedule

for today. Is that still fine with you?" So often an amateur salesperson gets told halfway through a meeting that the time has been cut short—and the prospect takes control. The gold medal salesperson clarifies the time available. This allows the salesperson to tailor the approach to the meeting, to organise it into distinct segments, and to remain composed. Gold medal salespeople are able to keep control of the systematic approach appropriately within the agreed time constraints.

"I know we spoke before," Linda continues, "but what exactly would you like to achieve from today's meeting?" If there are multiple people in the meeting, the same powerful phrase can be used to attain the same result. "I want to make sure everyone gets the most out of today's meeting, so can I ask you individually what you are looking to achieve by the end of the meeting?" Listen carefully using active listening skills to what each person has said, and repeat back to them what it is they have said.

Linda then says, "Thank you for you sharing that with me. I will try to make sure that I address each of these matters during the course of the meeting. But are you OK knowing that this may involve a bit more homework on both sides?"

That question is so critical. Often the amateur salesperson makes an assumption regarding what the prospects want to achieve. However, they are often on completely different pages. The salesperson is then made aware at some juncture of the meeting—it can be right at the end—what the prospect wants.

It is then too late. The engagement has been wasted as there was no clarity between the parties.

The gold medal salesperson identifies at the beginning of the meeting exactly what the prospect is seeking to have answered. This sets the gold medal salesperson apart, as the prospect is happy that the salesperson has listened to the requirements and dealt with them appropriately. It establishes bonding and rapport between the two parties and, most importantly, trust. The gold medal salesperson is now on the road to becoming a trusted advisor to the prospect.

A true gold medal salesperson like Linda recognises that there are three types of prospects in this world. These are time wasters, information gatherers, and real prospects. The gold medal salesperson is able to ascertain what type of prospect each is by the response to the "homework" question. Time wasters and information gatherers are always uncomfortable with the question of reciprocity, and from their body language and syntax, the gold medal salesperson can identify if this is the case. True prospects, on the other hand, welcome questions and reciprocity since they finally have someone who is taking the time to understand their requirements and what matters to them.

"I really hope we can help you," Linda continues, "but we are not right for everyone. So is it all right that I am going to need to ask you some questions in order to determine whether I can meet your expectations? I am sure you also have many questions for me." This clearly draws the line in the sand that Linda will not do premature presentations or engage in features-and-benefits selling. The fact that the gold medal salesperson is not willing to be forced to pitch without thoroughly understanding the requirements of the prospect differentiates them from the amateur. This is a very authentic step and incorporates the use of reverse psychology. Although it is honest, prospects find it very disarming. They then view the gold medal salesperson differently from the amateur salesperson, who often promises the world in an effort to get a deal. This candor results in the prospect feeling secure and valuing the gold medal salesperson as someone who is worthy of trust.

Linda then sets the final expectations. "So I guess at the end of our meeting one of three things is going to happen. You may decide that this is not something you want to pursue any further. If this is the case, please tell me and I won't be offended in any way. Or, if for some reason I don't think that we are the best company to help you, I will let you know and I hope you will be OK with that. Finally, we may find there is a good fit, and we can work on some next steps together."

In most traditional sale interactions, next steps are always discussed at the end of the meeting. This normally results in the prospect telling the salesperson to wait for a response. Once again, time wasters and information gatherers hate this idea of stating three possible endings since all they want is more information and free consulting. True prospects are open to agreeing to these three options since they have already articulated what they want from the meeting and will be happy if you, the salesperson, can effectively solve their particular business needs.

Up-Front Contracts Make Cold Calls Work

The traditional cold call starts with the amateur salesperson saying, "Hi, I am Jim from Company XYZ. The reason I am calling is to see if you are interested in exploring the insurance options for your company. Did you know you can save—" That is when the prospect generally hangs up (or, if you're lucky, disengages politely). The amateur salesperson made the mistake of launching into their pitch immediately without any consultation with the prospect.

Linda, the gold medal salesperson, begins her cold calls with the simple up-front contract. "Hi, I am Linda from Company ABC. Please excuse me. I know you are not expecting my call. Have I caught you at a bad time or in the middle of something?"

Linda then waits for a response. If the prospect is busy, she apologises and says, "Don't worry, I will call you later. Is there a time that is best to reach you?" We find that on average 80% of people who are approached in this manner respond with, "No, that is all right. What is this about?" The next part of this up-front contract from Linda is, "Would it be helpful if I tell you the reason I am calling?" Saying this indicates that you value the prospect's time and are being very non-pushy. It results in the prospect being much more receptive to the discussion going forward. The up-front contract increases the clarity and mutual understanding between these two entities.

Gold medal salespeople like Linda know that up-front contracts are vital components of a successful sales interaction that must be used consistently and effectively with prospects and clients alike.

Reflections

Up-front contracts save you time and money because you qualify out time wasters and information gatherers early in the process. As with other powerful techniques, when implemented carefully, the application of up-front contracts generates an awesome ROI for professional salespeople. Just as Muhammad Ali did in the boxing ring, you can assume strategic control of your process using these and similar strategies.

SALES MUSCLE #7

No Pain, No Win

"I've grown most not from victories, but setbacks. If winning is God's reward, then losing is how he teaches us."

—Serena Williams

SERENA WILLIAMS has dominated her sport, women's tennis, like no athlete alive. She has won four Olympic gold medals, one in women's singles and three in women's doubles—an all-time record that she shares with her sister, Venus. While her 23 singles titles (at the time of writing, that's six Wimbledons, seven Australian Opens, seven U.S. Opens and three French Opens) put her second place behind Margaret Court (24) on the all-time list, she is widely acknowledged as the greatest female player in tennis history. A big reason for this is the astonishing fact that she is, as this book goes to press, still ranked in the top 10 worldwide, 24 years after her professional debut in 1995. That's a remarkable career. Some call her "Serena the Great," others the "Fierce Stomping Diva." Many call her simply the greatest female athlete ever.

Williams's emotions drive her. She wears them on her sleeve, whether she is winning or losing.

"You fight!" Serena Williams screamed to herself after reaching championship point at the 2017 Australian Open final to win #23. "I really wanted to get to 23 so bad," Williams told ESPN after the match. "More than you can ever imagine!" Her ferocious drive to break new sports barriers is beyond question. Yet, what motivates her as much as her drive to win is, as Williams herself puts it, her "hatred of losing."

Whether it is a game of cards or a French Open first round loss, Williams mourns every loss. But losing only makes her a better opponent for her next challenger. Whenever she loses a match, she heads right back to the courts for practice, to train harder—to create a defense against the attack that defeated her.

Who can forget the sight of Williams, in major trouble during her three-set semifinal win in the 2015 French Open over Timea Baczinszky, wrapping herself in ice towels during changeovers, wheezing between points, the ordeal etched on her face. She had come down with the flu early on in the tournament.

"I think about it a lot, and I still don't know how I got

through it," Williams has said. "My eyes were glassy, and I was just not doing well." But she used her emotional commitment to not losing to will herself to win that semi-final. She then skipped practice on finals day, preferring to rest up at her Paris apartment, and then pulled herself out of a mid-match slump to beat Lucie Safarova in three sets—to clinch her twentieth Grand Slam title.

More recently Williams won her twenty-third singles grand slam tennis title at the 2017 Australian Open while eight weeks pregnant—what an amazing achievement.

Bottom line: Williams cannot bear to be beaten by her competition. This is often what differentiates the Olympic-level athlete from the amateur. It is the emotional drive to be the best—the drive to not be second to anyone.

Amateur Athletes Not Emotionally Connected to Winning

For amateur athletes, the drive to win or not lose is important, but hardly paramount. They are not emotionally connected to the result in the way that gold medal athletes are.

For amateur athletes, other factors about playing sports assume more importance, such as the social elements: engaging with others, having fun, or enjoying the camaraderie that is so often part of playing a group sport. However, amateur athletes are also prone to being easily distracted or diverted. They do not train or prepare physically and mentally in the same way as gold medal athletes. The result of a game or match does not have the same emotional impact as it does for those competing at the highest level.

Prospects Buy Emotionally, But Decide Intellectually

It's clear that Williams's emotional connection to winning and losing, as much as her natural talent and dedication, drive her to be the best she can be. So how does this relate to effective selling?

"Pain" in the gold medal sales system is defined as the emotional connection to the gap between where prospects are now and where they want to be (in relation to the product or service that could solve their challenge or problem).

Think about the way you buy. Whether your purchase is as simple as satisfying your need for a sweet treat or driven by your internal need to buy a safe product to protect your family, it's usually an emotional response that has you open your wallet.

The sad truth is that if you can't get prospects emotionally connected to what is most important to them, it's likely that you will face a long sales cycle—or end up with a slow *no*. Moreover, a lot of time and energy will have been wasted that could have been spent with someone more qualified to purchase from you—if only you had followed a gold medal sales process that involved uncovering whether there was pain or not.

So, the prospect must be emotionally involved in the sale, and the pain must affect the prospect on an emotional level.

After the emotional decision has been made to buy, the prospect then justifies the buying decision intellectually.

When uncovering pain, you move the prospect from the general to the specific—from the surface problem to the underlying reason, and only then to the business and personal impacts of pain.

Uncovering pain involves:

- Discerning the issues underneath the surface of the prospect's needs (the *what*).
- Discovering the cause of these issues (the *why*).
- Determining how these issues are impacting the business and how they are personally impacting the prospect (the *how*).
- Qualifying whether the prospect is actually willing and prepared to do anything to solve the problem/challenge the business is facing.

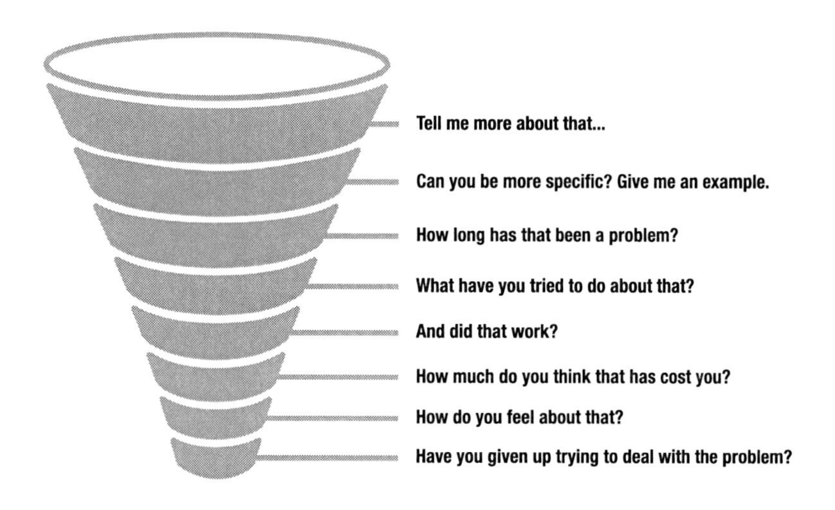

The Sandler Pain Funnel® is a technique used for questioning a prospect. Unlike in features-and-benefits selling, the prospect is led through a series of questions to uncover the prospect's present pain. The more that is uncovered, the deeper the questions that can be asked.

During a sales conversation, only when the full extent of the prospect's pain has been reached does the gold medal salesperson offer solutions. Even then, the salesperson asks the prospect questions to reinforce willingness to accept the solutions—which forces the prospect to make a decision whether to continue the interaction on the salesperson's terms or to exit it.

With the Pain Funnel, the salesperson guides the prospect through questions that lead to the pain that the prospect may currently be experiencing—or attempting to avoid.

Proper application of the Pain Step (explained in detail in Chapter 8) requires discipline to learn and understand the eight-step Pain Funnel questioning process. It also requires a generous serving of creativity, as every prospect will have different challenges and different ways of communicating and being.

Fumiko Conducts the Pain Process

Let's look at how Fumiko, a gold medal salesperson who sells customer relationship management (CRM) software, conducts the pain process.

Fumiko receives a call from a potential client with a financial services company that employs over a hundred people. She schedules a brief exploratory phone call with the caller, whom she takes through a systematic mini-qualification process to establish whether the lead is a prospect or not.

Once she knows the lead is a qualified prospect, Fumiko sets up a face-to-face meeting. At the beginning of the meeting, she establishes her up-front contract (covered in detail in the previous chapter) to ensure absolute clarity between all parties at the meeting. This also reinforces equal business stature throughout all subsequent sales interactions.

This up-front contract confirms that Fumiko has permission to ask the questions she needs answered, which safeguards her from being pushed into talking about the features and benefits of her services too early. (As a gold medal salesperson, Fumiko does not present her solutions prematurely in the sales process.)

Fumiko's 30-Second Commercial

In order to initiate the pain process, Fumiko first delivers a 30-Second Commercial, which is essentially a powerful third-party testimonial conversation. Buyers tend to respond positively to such a testimonial, as they are likely to relate to and identify with the challenges of the company that has provided the testimonial.

Below is an example of the 30-second commercial that Fumiko uses.

"Typically when I speak to marketing directors like yourself, they often tell me that they have a great list of contacts but it is difficult to access them efficiently. Or, they have these contacts stored in different formats like spreadsheets or written down, but they are not stored all in one place. Thus valuable company information can be lost."

Fumiko then follows her commercial with the following question:

"I don't suppose you experience any of this in your world?"

This is a Negative Reverse Selling®* tactic, designed to obtain a truthful *yes* or *no* from the prospect. Fumiko then gently guides the prospect through a series of questions to uncover the reasons the company may need the service she is offering, namely the CRM system.

She puts her prospects at ease by using softening statements between questions, taking care to ensure that the prospect does not feel interrogated at any stage during the pain questioning process. Examples of such softening statements and questions Fumiko may pose are below.

"I hear this from a lot of clients."
"Can I ask you a tough question?"
"That is not unusual for me to hear."
"I understand."

---

* Source: David Sandler.

At the end of this pain questioning, both Fumiko and the prospect have a deep understanding of where the prospect's real problem lies. Moreover, since Fumiko has uncovered these pains without trying to sell anything to the prospect, a strong bond has been established between Fumiko (the gold medal salesperson) and the prospect. The prospect now has a greater degree of trust in Fumiko as a true trusted advisor. Also, the prospect is likely to want to move quickly to resolve the self-articulated problems that have been uncovered during the meeting, namely, to make the sale happen.

Fumiko understands that when prospects are only intellectually connected to their problems, moving forward quickly is unlikely. Typically, prospects do nothing—because the proposed solution does not affect their emotional state or wellbeing.

Fumiko has a good grasp of the functional aspects of the CRM, and she understands the features and benefits of the software. However, unlike an amateur salesperson, she waits until the prospect is deeply connected to the exact nature of the company's specific requirements and challenges before presenting her recommendations.

This means that when Fumiko presents her solution, she will tailor it to solve the prospect's particular needs and requirements, and thus mostly likely close the sale.

Amateur Hour

Compare Fumiko's approach to that of Stu, an amateur salesperson.

Stu is a features-and-benefits expert for his software product. We like to compare this type of salesperson with that well-worn stereotype, the used-car salesperson, who spouts long monologues about things like "low mileage" and "fuel efficiency" without ever connecting with the buyer on an emotional level. Let's take a look at Stu's sales process.

Stu receives a call from an insurance company expressing interest in purchasing CRM software. He is excited and immediately sets up the meeting. He says that he is free to take the meeting on whatever day or time suits the prospect. Stu may not know it, but he is behaving in a desperate manner.

Unlike Fumiko, who sets up a preliminary phone call to ensure that she is going to visit a real prospect, Stu puts his valuable time at risk by possibly going to meet a time waster or information gatherer prospect.

Stu arrives at the face-to-face meeting and engages in the usual chitchat that he assumes is effective communication, but is, in fact, cementing his status as the amateur traditional salesperson that he is—and is certainly not creating equal business stature.

At the meeting outset, Stu does not deliver an up-front contract. Without it, no ground rules have been set to ensure clarity between all parties at the meeting. Stu has also not confirmed that he can ask the questions he needs answered before he presents a solution—which ensures he is likely to be pushed into talking about the features and benefits of his services too early.

The meeting begins. The prospect quickly takes control of the meeting, outlining the company's challenges to Stu. It should also be noted here that without an effective Pain Step (entirely missing from Stu's arsenal of amateur sales tools), the challenges the prospect has outlined to Stu may in fact not be the real challenges the company is facing.

Stu (who does present early in the sales process), quickly powers up his laptop to excitedly demonstrate all the features and benefits of his product. Stu knows very little about the real needs of the prospect, so—surprise, surprise—Stu is doing all the talking. When he is worn-out from all this chatter, Stu asks the prospect, "What do you think?"

The prospect politely responds, saying something like, "It looks very interesting. Could you send me a detailed proposal, please, Stu? We are likely to move on this very quickly."

After Stu has left the building, the prospect puts a call through to the front-desk person, saying: "Do not, in any circumstances, put through any calls from him, and please don't waste my time dealing with salespeople who don't listen to what we are looking for and just show up and throw up."

Poor Stu! He left the meeting in high excitement. "Wow! What a lasting impression I made!" Sadly, Stu made a lasting impression all right, but it was a terrible one. It is a fact that traditional features-and-benefits selling rarely, if ever, works effectively.

However, all of this is lost on Stu, who rushes back to his office and recounts what happened at his "incredible meeting" to his sales director. "This is going to be one huge deal that will really put the company on the map," he jokes. "You'll be signing me the biggest commission check ever!"

A-Player Salesperson Elena Smashes the Sales Record (Serena-Style!)

To close this chapter, here's an example of an A-Player employee who can teach you many things about what it takes to succeed.

Elena had just arrived in London with no prior experience in the market into which she was selling. However, she had amazing ambition and drive, which she attributed to her deep emotional connection to winning. This, she said, gave her an insatiable desire to succeed—and succeed she did. Within nine months she had broken all company sales records. Her sales were 300% higher than the next top-performing salesperson.

Elena overcame all objections and problems that amateur salespeople would use as excuses to justify why they did not hit their targets, such as, "The marketing literature is ineffective," or, "Their competition's product is better than ours," or, "No one has the budget in this economy."

Unlike the amateur salesperson Stu, Elena did not rely on the features and benefits of her services. Instead, she used skillful sales techniques and effective communication skills to connect her prospects to the problems and pains they were facing. She then showed them how she could resolve them with her service offering.

Reflection

Selling through using pain sets gold medal salespeople apart from amateur salespeople. However, it requires the careful study and application of pain questions, and it requires strong discipline to not fall into the traditional features-and-benefits trap. In many ways, the Pain Step is the most important part of the powerful seven-step sales process described in detail in the next chapter.

SALES MUSCLE #8

Lead the Dance

"It doesn't just come overnight. You've got to train for it and believe in yourself; that's the most important thing."

—Mo Farah

MO FARAH is the only British athlete to earn gold medals for running in three successive Olympics competitions, winning all three men's 10,000m race titles. Moreover, after winning the 10,000m race in Rio de Janeiro in 2016, he recovered and went on to win the 5,000m gold as well. (He also won the 5,000m gold in Beijing.) He is, in short, the most decorated and highest achieving British athlete in history.

So what makes Mo Farah special in the world of running? Is it his genetics, his innate skill and talent, or his desire to be the best? In truth, according to him, it is his training. Of course, he also has a slender frame and lean muscle tone—an ideal physical structure for an endurance runner or athlete. Farah also has a flowing and energy-efficient gait and running style. But that wouldn't make him a champion without the preparation and discipline of his training.

As an Olympian and World Champion, Farah has applied systems in all aspects of his life successfully. These systems are all focused on maximising his running performance. His activities are simple: eat; train; rest. Farah is vigilant with his diet to allow for optimum nutritional intake and to provide sufficient metabolic energy for his grueling physical training.

Farah also spends hours on the road perfecting his running technique and strengthening the endurance capabilities of his muscular and cardiovascular systems. His lungs and heart must be strong, his running form fluid—and he must have stores of energy to call upon while he is running against the world's top athletes. Farah has trained and applied his methods of perfecting his performance to the point where he has built up confidence and belief in his abilities. In short, he trusts himself to be at his best because of his systems, which have been proven time and time again to be effective.

Sales Systems

Having an effective system is just as important for a gold medal sales approach.

There are only two sales systems out there: professional and amateur. Which one are you following? The defining difference between the approach and preparation of amateurs versus gold medal salespeople is that the latter use a system to enable them to perform at their optimum level as well as maintain the discipline to stick to this system. Gold medal salespeople have a system and stick to it; amateurs do as they please.

Think of how amateur athletes compete. It is all for fun. Winning is the aim of course, but there is no system in place that has been thought through and applied rigorously in the pursuit of victory. For example, let's think of half-marathon runners who run regularly in the week. They are happy to have a beer with their friends when they feel like it. If they miss a run that is all right. A burger here or there as the desire arises doesn't matter. What matters is that they are able to maintain a healthy lifestyle to the point that they are active and are able to finish the events in which they participate with ease.

Now let's think of the gold medal Olympic athlete's approach to performance. Let's use a competitive marathon runner. In preparation for an upcoming competition, many Olympic athletes train at high altitudes in order to increase the mitochondrial content in their blood. This in turn increases the oxidative conversion capacity of their red blood cells. The result is boosted performance.

Gold medal athletes also have trainers who are well-versed in human kinetics, muscle physiology, and psychology for the purpose of improving their athlete's performance.

Moreover, gold medal athletes have spent years of their lives training daily and applying a systematic approach to all aspects of their lives. In effect, they have put so many miles under their feet that they have essentially circumnavigated the earth in training—for the purpose of being able to push themselves beyond their previous best.

In short, gold medal athletes have a system that they follow.

Buyer-Seller Dance

One of the two systems that salespeople apply when they sell works. The other doesn't.

Let's take the first, known as the Buyer-Seller Dance. This is the system that most amateur salespeople follow.

THE SALESPERSON:

1. Gets a meeting with a prospect
2. Presents the solution
3. Tries to close
4. Chases

WHILE THE BUYER:

1. Misleads or lies
2. Gets information
3. Commits to nothing
4. Goes into hiding

Ronin's Prospect Takes the Lead in the Buyer-Seller Dance

The scenario below recounts the experience of Ronin, a marketing consultant, engaging in the Buyer-Seller Dance as he tries to sell his services.

Ronin receives a call from a leading IT company. The caller tells Ronin that the contacts at the company want to overhaul their marketing strategy, and they have heard great things about Ronin's marketing services. They'd like him to come and see them since they want to move quickly to work with him if they can agree on terms together.

Ronin is very excited and flattered by their interest and takes a two-hour train journey to attend the meeting. At this meeting, the company's marketing manager tells Ronin that the company wants a total marketing revamp. He then asks Ronin if he can provide an outline of how he would go about this and to share a range of different options of how he could market the company more effectively.

The marketing manager asks Ronin to put all this information into a written proposal and implies that if he is happy with Ronin's proposal, the company will give the green light on this work and get going as soon as possible. In reality, the company is either shopping around for different quotes, which will then be used to beat the incumbent supplier, or the marketing manager is simply gathering information from a variety of suppliers—like Ronin. Simply, the marketing manager is misleading Ronin—lying to him, in fact, and the company is actually quite unlikely to use his marketing services.

An upbeat Ronin leaves the meeting so motivated that he spends three days (and three nights!) creating a cross-platform marketing approach that he feels will exceed all the marketing manager's expectations. He tells all his colleagues (and anyone else who will listen) about his new client. Unfortunately this is not a client, but a prospect—leading Ronin to a merry dance, with Ronin blissfully unaware of the unfolding situation.

Ronin sends the proposal to the company and receives an email from the marketing manager saying: "Thank you so much for the proposal—it looks brilliant! We will come back to you very soon with our feedback." Ronin is so excited about this "sure fire" deal (and all the money he is going to make) that he splashes out on a new suit and books himself and his wife on a two-week trip to Hawaii—flying business class.

A week passes, and Ronin has still not heard back from the marketing manager. Ronin is not worried. He is sure the company's management team is probably very busy digesting all the intricacies and different options that he put together in his 100-page proposal. Another two weeks pass. Radio silence from the marketing manager. Ronin, now slightly worried, puts in a call to the marketing manager. The manager is very polite and says he will get back to Ronin on Friday. Friday comes, and lo and behold, there is no call from the marketing manager.

The following Monday Ronin calls again and is told that the

marketing manager is now on a two-week vacation, and Ronin should call back in two weeks' time. Ronin is now frantic! He tries to cancel his two-week trip to Hawaii, but the booking is fully non-refundable. Ronin buries his head in the sand, hoping that in two weeks all will be well and the deal will be done with the IT company.

Two weeks later Ronin calls again, and is told that the marketing manager is busy, but he will call Ronin back. Again, no response, and no call back either. Ronin then decides to email the marketing manager, asking when the company will be ready to give the green light. Two days later Ronin receives a polite email from the marketing manager saying: "Thank you so much for your time and effort, but the marketing director has put this job on hold for six months. Could you please call us back in in six months' time when we will revisit this project? We look forward to speaking at that time."

Welcome to the Buyer-Seller Dance. Ronin's experience may sound extreme, but this is what actually happens to most salespeople on a regular basis. While this approach does occasionally lead to some sales, what is always true is that these salespeople are in a compliant relationship in which the buyer controls the seller and leads the sales process.

It is evident in the dynamic just described that the buyer (the marketing manager) is in control, leading the dance, while Ronin, the seller, is allowing himself to do the will of the marketing manager in the hope of securing a deal. The energy and intellectual effort of the amateur salesperson is squandered, which leads to mediocre sales results at best.

The amateur salesperson's pipeline is full of promising deals that appear to be in a stage of closing, yet always seem to struggle to materialise. It is so easy to become demoralised if this is your regular reality. As the sales cycle keeps lengthening and "clients" become radio silent, salespeople often exhibit desperation. No one is going to buy from a desperate salesperson.

Margo Follows a Gold Medal Sales System

Let's now take a look at the sales system that Margo, a gold medal salesperson, has been trained to follow.

First, Margo uses a systematic approach in which there is equal business stature between the salesperson and the prospect, and she holds the belief in a win-win relationship—or no deal. Margo also recognises the need to qualify early on in the sales process to weed out non-opportunities, as well as choosing to only work with prospects who have properly qualified. The sales system Margo uses is known as the Sandler Submarine.

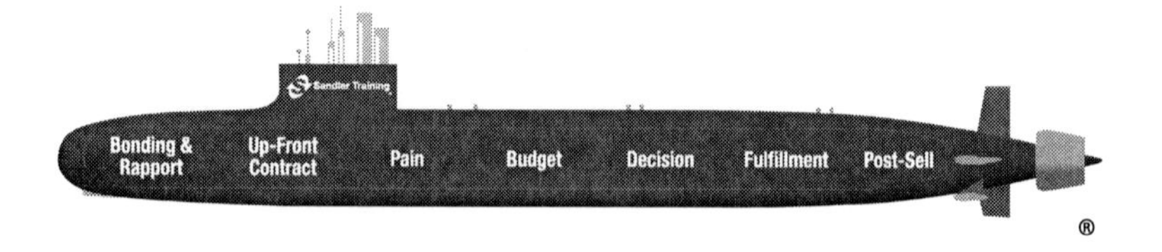

Step 1: Bonding & Rapport

Margo understands the importance of making prospects feel comfortable and knows that people have different styles of communication. She is aware of communicating in the style of her prospect, rather than interacting with the prospect using her own communication style. Margo is skilled at interacting with people on a professional level, and she realises that people only buy from people they like and trust. Her personality style is both nurturing and assertive.

This is in contrast to many other salespeople, who engage in inconsequential chitchat and are often desperate or subservient to the potential buyer, Margo creates a relationship of equal business stature, based on trust and mutual respect.

Margo also understands that most prospects expect a Buyer-Seller Dance experience, whether they are conscious of this or not. This sets the tone of the relationship and the ground rules for the future interaction. Margo knows that it is vital to lead the dance.

How does she do this? She uses the up-front contract.

Step 2: Up-Front Contract

By using an up-front contract (also discussed in Chapter 6), Margo lets the marketing manager prospect know that she follows a systematic sales process with all potential new clients.

In every interaction Margo has with the marketing manager, there is always equal business stature.

Margo is clear that in every conversation or sales meeting there is mutual agreement. Moreover, there are always three potential outcomes to each meeting:

1. The marketing manager is always given the opportunity to say no at the end of any sales meeting. This demonstrates a very respectful attitude toward the marketing manager, unlike the amateur salesperson, who is always pushing for a *yes*, which often results in the prospect lying because they feel so pressured.
2. Margo lets the marketing manager know that if at any time she feels the interaction is not progressing in a win-win manner, she will very respectfully bring the sales conversation to a polite end.
3. There have to be mutually-agreed-upon next steps for Margo to be willing to invest further time in interacting with the marketing manager.

The use of this up-front contract sets Margo apart from her competition, as she looks and acts like a true trusted advisor. This means that she will first ask the marketing manager a series of questions to truly gain an understanding of the company's needs.

Margo then moves on to the next step of her systematic sales process—pain.

STEP 3: PAIN

In the Pain Step, Margo helps the prospect uncover the gap between where the prospect is now and where the prospect wants to be. Margo uses third-party stories to which the marketing manager can relate to initiate the Pain Step.

For example, Margo might say: "Typically, when I speak to other marketing managers like yourself, they tell me one of three things: first, they have a very innovative product that they sell, but they are battling to get in front of enough qualified prospects; second, the marketing team is very hard-working, but individuals are battling to get consistent results; or third, they are under pressure from the business to deliver more with less resources. I don't suppose you face anything like this?"

Margo understands that people buy emotionally, so it is important to get the prospect connected emotionally before she even gets close to presenting any potential solution to the prospect's problem. With a systematic process, she takes the marketing manager from intellectual connection to the relevant problems to an emotional connection with the pain that will be solved.

Once the prospect is emotionally connected to the problem, only then are they really committed to solving the problem. (Generally, the prospect wants the problem solved quickly by a salesperson like Margo, who is a trusted advisor, whom the prospect respects.)

This Pain Step contrasts very strongly to traditional features-and-benefits selling that an amateur salesperson like Ronin practices. Moreover, in the Pain Step Margo also helps the prospect uncover the impact of the problem—and the cost to the business. Last, but not least, Margo also helps the prospect identify how the problem is impacting them personally.

If Margo has done this, she has gone a long way towards qualifying the prospect. Now the prospect wants to buy from her to solve the problem. They are now very keen for Margo to present a solution. However, Margo knows that unless she qualifies them for the next two steps (Budget and Decision), she could be in for a Buyer-Seller Dance, just like Ronin. She values her time too highly to allow this to happen.

So before she goes to the next steps, Margo understands the need to use some reverse psychology to get the prospect to open up to Budget and Decision questions—prior to presenting a solution.

This is why she now says: "We have helped many clients with this type of problem before, but we are not necessarily a good fit for everybody. Before I show you a potential solution to your problem and maybe put a proposal together for you, can I share with you two reasons why we sometimes can't help people?"

Margo now moves to the first reason, which is the Budget Step.

STEP 4: BUDGET

In the Budget Step, Margo says to the prospect: "There are some commitments that we require from any potential client before we work with them."

First, there's a time investment. Margo goes into detail about this, asking the marketing manager if they would be willing to invest in this time frame in order to solve the problem.

Second, Margo says: "There may be some resources required to solve the problem, e.g., the marketing director's input may be required or the financial director's input may be required. Would that be possible?"

Third, Margo would say: "There's a certain amount of vitality and energy required for us to work well together." Margo now sets up the money question—one that most traditional salespeople avoid. She asks the marketing manager: "Assuming I can show you something that you like that will solve your problem, what sort of budget do we have to work with to solve this problem?"

She uses excellent communication skills, perhaps interjecting a playful style here, e.g., "I guess we now have to talk about that big, bad monster—money."

Using this playful communication style, Margo is able to get the prospect to share, in a very non-confrontational Adult-to-Adult manner, the company's investment criteria. (Margo's bonding and rapport skills ensure that she does not come across as pushy and desperate when she asks these budget qualification questions.)

Unlike Ronin, the amateur salesperson, Margo has skillfully understood—before she even moved to the proposal stage—that the marketing manager is now willing and able to make the appropriate budget commitments required to purchase Margo's services. This Budget Step is the second part of the qualification process.

Margo now moves onto the third part of the process—the Decision Step.

STEP 5: DECISION

In this step (the second reason that Margo's company is sometimes not the right fit), she will again use highly effective communication. This will enable her to ask potentially difficult questions that the amateur salesperson would have left out; e.g., Ronin is likely to have assumed that the prospect (the marketing manager) would have made all the right decisions and be willing to move forward in regard to purchasing Ronin's services.

Margo understands that the Decision Step could also be called the Stakeholder Step because this is the step in which Margo sets out to discover who all the relevant stakeholders are: those directly involved with and other key decision makers for purchasing Margo's marketing services.

Margo would ask a question such as: "Before I put together

a proposal for you to consider, could I ask you who are all the relevant stakeholders that might be impacted by us potentially working together?" This question allows the prospect to consider all the relevant decision makers, from the executive level down to junior staff.

By asking all these questions in the Decision Step, Margo further cements her position as a trusted advisor while maintaining her equal business stature.

Margo also understands some of the other killer questions she needs to have answered before she writes a proposal, such as: "Assuming I put together a proposal that meets your needs, what would your time frame be for making a decision like this?" "When would the project actually start?" Probably the most important question to ask is: "Can I ask you a tough question? Whose signature goes on the check to sign off on this type of project?"

At the end of the Decision Step, Margo has taken the marketing manager through a series of three qualification steps:

- The Pain Step
- The Budget Step
- The Decision Step

Margo will only move to the Fulfillment Step if the above three steps have been concluded successfully. This ensures that Margo has a deeply qualified prospect before she prepares a presentation.

Unlike amateur salesperson Ronin, by following the first five steps of the Sandler sales process Margo avoids being drawn into the Buyer-Seller Dance. This allows Margo to devote most of her time and effort into following a consistent and effective prospecting plan.

Step 6: Fulfillment

Margo understands that she still needs to follow a very systematic Fulfillment Step—not the typical "show up and throw up" presentation step Ronin adopted. Before Margo presents her solution to the marketing manager she performs the following review.

She reviews the Pain, Budget, and Decision Step answers that the marketing manager has given her to ensure nothing has been missed and there is clarity on all sides. She also sets an ultimate up-front contract: Before she presents her solution, she lets the marketing manager know the process she will follow and also the potential next steps.

Margo then presents the solution to the prospect; i.e., her presentation is aligned with what was revealed in the Pain, Budget, and Decision Steps. Margo performs a thermometer close, which is a question such as: "On a scale of 1 to 10, how comfortable are you that I have addressed the problems or the challenges you have shared with me?" (Any score under 6 would mean that Margo had missed something in her solution. However, she could still rectify this situation by asking a question such as: "What would I need to add to get me closer to a 10?")

Assuming that the previous point is concluded successfully, Margo confirms the sale with a question: "What would you like me to do next?" Margo has now done what Ronin, the amateur salesperson, could not do. She has influenced the marketing manager to make a buying decision—not pressured the marketing manager with a hard sell, which most buyers do not like.

Margo recognises there is still one more step to perform (even though she has closed the sale)—the Post-Sell Step.

STEP 7: POST-SELL

In the Post-Sell Step, Margo has two functions to perform.

1. AVERT BUYER'S REMORSE.

For example, Margo is likely to be replacing an incumbent supplier. She is aware of this—unlike Ronin. Margo also knows that the incumbent supplier is unlikely to send her a bowl of red roses to congratulate her on taking the account.

So Margo asks a question such as: "I'm assuming you have an incumbent supplier that I am replacing. But can I ask you—what is going to happen if that supplier comes back to you and says they will undercut me to retain your business?"

Essentially, Margo is coaching the prospective client on how to handle such a future situation. Margo has averted a possible scenario with which many amateur salespeople fail to deal.

2. Ensure a steady stream of qualified introductions.

Margo understands that money does grow on trees—on introduction trees. Moreover, the best time to ask the question about introductions is when a sale has just closed.

Margo would again use careful communication to ask a question such as: "I hope you don't mind if I ask one more thing? If this question makes you feel uncomfortable, please let me know. The question is: A lot of our new clients come from existing clients. Would you mind—in a few months, assuming the project is going well—if I asked you if there were any other marketing managers in your network you might possibly introduce me to for an exploratory conversation?"

Because Margo has behaved like a true professional throughout the sales process, most prospects will be 100% comfortable when asked this question.

Reflection

Becoming a gold medal salesperson requires a professional attitude, hard work, and the discipline to stick to an effective system. There are only two systems out there for the seller and the buyer to engage in: 1) the Buyer-Seller Dance, or 2) the seven-step Sandler sales process.

The good news is that while not everyone can become Mo Farah and win gold medals at three consecutive Olympics, with a disciplined approach and by following the sales system outlined in this book, most people can all become trusted advisors—i.e., successful salespeople.

SALES MUSCLE #9

Achieve Your Personal Best

"What I missed in the pros was playing with a coherent philosophy, as we did for Coach Wooden."

—Walt Hazzard

JOHN WOODEN, one of the most influential and revered coaches in the history of sports, was and remains a powerful voice on "personalising the process in order to maximise performance," both on and off the basketball court. UCLA Bruins guard Walt Hazzard's success as a player and a coach was built entirely on Wooden's system. All of that explains why this chapter takes such a close look at Coach Wooden.

Hazzard, a talented guard also known as Mahdi Abdul-Rahman, played basketball in college for the UCLA Bruins and was a member of their first national championship team. He won a gold medal in 1964 as a member of the U.S. team at the 1964 Summer Olympics.

Although Hazzard went on to an All-Star pro career in the NBA, and then served as coach of the UCLA team, he's in this chapter for one reason and one reason alone: his willingness to follow the enduring example of his mentor, the great coach John Wooden. Hazzard's success in the 1964 Olympics (and afterwards) is inconceivable without Wooden's influence, his coaching philosophy, and his process.

Hazzard was the key playmaker on the first of Wooden's legendary championship teams at UCLA. Of his time playing under Coach Wooden, Hazzard once said, "I liked winning a championship, being considered a champion, but looking back, back at UCLA, I'm even prouder of the attitude we established there. ... Nobody ever expected us to win (as the season began), but we knew we were never out of it if we stayed together. That was the attitude. We were so sharp, so determined. You knew everybody would be there."

The 1964 UCLA squad came, seemingly out of nowhere, to win 30 consecutive games, post an undefeated season, and claim the school's first national championship. Wooden would eventually lead UCLA squads to an unheard of ten national championships in twelve years. Anyone who knows anything about men's college basketball knows that John Wooden was that sport's most successful coach, and Hazzard's contributions to the 1964 gold medal effort gives Wooden a claim to at least some of the credit for the U.S. team's Olympic success, as well.

It is worth noting here that as a coach, Hazzard followed closely in his mentor's footsteps and, as a result, led the 1985 UCLA squad to an NIT championship. This speaks to the powerful tradition of excellence that Hazzard inherited from the remarkable man who had coached him two decades earlier.

The "Wizard of Westwood," as Wooden was known, was a three-time All-American player in his youth at Purdue. He is the only man who has been inducted into the Basketball Hall of Fame as both a player and a coach.

During the 1960s and 1970s, Wooden led the UCLA Bruins to unparalleled levels of success. They posted seven consecutive season championships, and at one point Wooden's squads had posted 88 unbeaten games in a row. In four seasons, UCLA suffered no defeat. They were literally unbeatable over that period of time. In his 27 years leading the Bruins, his record stands at 620-147 games won-lost, a staggering win ratio. How did Wooden achieve all this? What was his key to unlocking the potential of his players? Wooden's 15 Building Blocks on his so-called "Pyramid of Success" provide the answer. The system is now implemented in teams from many different sports and even in corporate boardrooms. In it, Wooden lists the qualities that are requisite to ensuring personal—not just on-the-court—success. These qualities include industriousness, self-control, loyalty, friendship, enthusiasm, and competitive greatness. He trusted this 15-point system and followed it rigidly.

Most observers (then and now), however, have looked for

a single, concise answer to the question, "What did Coach Wooden do differently?" The simplest answer to this question can be found in one of John Wooden's great leadership lessons: Practice time is just as important as game time. His instructions to his players were that during a game, they were never to focus on the current score. Instead, they should simply execute the selected plays, focusing on the actions that they had rehearsed countless times during practice sessions.

This was no empty slogan. Wooden had no problem with the team if they lost the game—as long as they had executed the behaviours to the very best of their ability. By the same token, if one of his teams won a game while slacking off on the behaviours they had practiced, Wooden would let them know how he felt about their performance. The shift in perspective from checking on what has been achieved to honing in on the actions needed to perform up to full potential was (and is) the key to success. The score is incidental. Only the effort, the intention, and the behaviour, deployed as practiced relentlessly at its full potential, are under the player's control. Wooden really was less interested in the final outcome on the scoreboard than he was in each player's personal level of effort in executing the game plan for the team. One of his most famous quotes is, "Success comes from knowing that you did your best to become the best that you are capable of becoming." He meant it. He wanted the best from each individual player. And he wanted proof of that player's full commitment to making personal improvements in execution, in every single practice. He wanted every single player to do his best, regardless of the score, regardless of whether the effort came during a game or during a practice session.

> "Your best is good enough," he repeatedly told us. "Don't beat yourself, don't cheat yourself, don't short-change yourself. That's the worst kind of defeat you'll ever suffer, and you'll never get over it." —NBA Hall of Famer Bill Walton, remembering John Wooden's practice sessions

Gold Medal Salespeople Use Sales Templates

Each salesperson is unique. Thus, creating a personalised sales plan with the correct mix of prospecting activities, and then executing that plan to the very best of your ability, is vitally important.

Sales templating is defined as a set series of interactions and conversations that lead to a desired sales outcome. It is used by a salesperson or sales team to build a personalised, consistent sales process.

The result is an efficient, documented sales system that is personalised to each unique salesperson, well designed enough to measure on the behavioural level, and simple enough to accommodate change—for example, dynamic market conditions, competitor threats, and lessons learned. (Another of Coach

Wooden's famous quotes is, "Failure is not fatal, but failure to change might be.")

Building Your Sales Template

The first step is to document all sales interactions that make up the different stages of the sales process for your product or service. Below is an example of such interactions that make up a sales template.

1. Research 100 target companies and source a number of appropriate contacts.
2. Call/email/use LinkedIn to target the contacts in order to qualify them for a 15-minute prospecting call (or qualify them out).
3. During the prospecting call, qualify the prospect for first level pain. (As we saw in Chapter 8, pain is the gap between where the prospect currently is and where the prospect would like to be, i.e., what is important to the prospect.) On this call, also ask questions to qualify the prospect on budget and decision criteria. The result of this call is that the prospect is either qualified out or qualified in for a face-to-face meeting.
4. During the face-to-face meeting, qualify the prospect deeply for first, second, and third level pain, as well as conducting a much deeper exploration of the prospect's pain, budget, and decision criteria. The result of

the face-to-face meeting is that the prospect is either qualified for a proposal or qualified out (the file is then closed).

5. In the proposal phase, the solution offered is aligned to the discovered pain, budget, and decision criteria for that prospect, and there is a clear up-front contract in place for the next steps.
6. The next steps are: 1) The prospect becomes a client and there are mutually-agreed-upon next steps, or 2) The prospect decides not to proceed.

Sales Template: Single Decision Maker

ABC Health Insurance, a small company with 10 salespeople, sells to individuals. Two years ago, the company invested in digital marketing (online lead generation) to generate new selling opportunities by converting site visitors to prospects. The sales team did everything they were supposed to do, but two years later revenues were still stuck at £1 million annually.

The typical initial incoming interaction via this lead generation strategy would go something like this: The lead would call the company to speak to a salesperson, engage in lots and lots of questions about health insurance, and then trap the salesperson into the Buyer-Seller Dance by requesting more information, committing to nothing, and going into hiding. The lead would say something along the lines of: "Let me take a look at a quote, and I'll think about it." "You can send the quote to me. I'm the decision maker." "Hmm, that sounds interesting. Send me a brochure and call me back sometime next week."

The company managing director was so frustrated by the lack of success that he changed the digital strategy a few times, but there was still no improvement. By the time ABC stumbled upon the selling system highlighted in this book, the managing director knew nothing was working and a major overhaul was needed. The company invested in training and learned the foundations of the selling system. Three years later their revenues had increased to £3 million.

ABC's first step was to customise the system by creating a sales template, which included documenting the purpose of each sales interaction. It's a fact that a sales interaction with no purpose puts the prospect firmly in control. Moreover, many uncomfortable sales calls, presentations, and meetings derail because salespeople don't follow basic rules for properly setting the stage for the call. Thus ABC's sales template included documenting the purpose for each interaction to keep the salesperson and prospect on track.

What did ABC's sales template look like?

Step 1: The company used digital marketing to generate 10 incoming leads a day for each salesperson.

Step 2: Each salesperson conducted an initial five-minute qualification call for each incoming lead.

Purpose:

- To ensure that the salesperson would take control of the structure of the call—and stay in control of the interaction until the end of the call.
- To look and sound different from competitors, providing the salesperson with a clear competitive advantage.
- To avoid the salesperson getting drawn into writing proposals for any prospect who asked for one at this stage of the sales process.

Step 3: For qualified prospects, the salesperson would follow up with an in-depth fact-finding call, which would last about 30 minutes.

Purpose:

- To set ABC salespeople apart from the competition as trusted advisors by asking the prospect all the relevant and required questions in order to come up with a customised solution. This contrasts strongly with the generally shallow questioning of the traditional pushy amateur salesperson.
- To establish ABC as a premium solution provider with the associated premium pricing.
- To focus on effective bonding and rapport to make the prospect feel comfortable throughout the call. The length and quality of the call would build trust between the salesperson and the prospect. The probable result would be the prospect providing truthful answers to

budget and decision-making related questions asked by the salesperson.

Step 4: The salesperson would then present the solution to the prospect, based on the answers received from the fact-finding call (Step 3).

Purpose:

- To present the solution, the salesperson would set up a clear up-front contract to keep the interaction on track to lead to one of only two outcomes: "Yes" (with a mutually-agreed-upon next step) or "No" (the file is closed—ensuring the salesperson wastes no further time chasing the prospect). The setup of a clear up-front contract would eliminate the possibility of the buyer taking control, saying something like: "I'll think it over"—which perpetuates the traditional Buyer-Seller Dance followed by ABC's competitors.
- To deliver excellent conversion rates, enhanced by the ABC sales team's sound understanding of the theory of communication profiling. This provided them with a method to present their solution in a way that would make the prospect feel very comfortable, as the prospect would be communicated with in their own language, rather than in traditional sales-speak.

Step 5: Sign the legal agreements and make payments.

Purpose:

- To devise excellent up-front contracts to ensure absolute clarity between the prospect and the salesperson in regard to legal and payment details. This set of mutually-agreed-upon expectations would leave no room for delayed signing of agreements or late payments so that the salesperson would not have to waste valuable time chasing the prospect. Last but not least, the prospect has become a valued client who would leave with a strong impression of the excellent service they have received and would likely refer the company to other prospects.

Sales Template: Enterprise Selling Example

Consider the case of an IT integration services firm we will call Top Tier. The company had been in business for two years and had experienced modest growth, winning eight projects with small- to medium-sized clients and generating £4 million in annual revenues.

The principals of the firm were eager to win a deal with a large enterprise client—a deal that could be a game changer, accelerating growth and propelling the young firm to higher levels. But they had no experience in pursuing or winning business from large enterprise prospects. Although the rewards were much greater, the risks were much higher as well, with greater consequences. Nonetheless, they were determined to make it happen.

While their modest growth over the two years had been largely the result of referrals from their small- to medium-sized clients, in order to achieve their enterprise objective, the principals embarked on a campaign to obtain RFPs for big deals with much larger clients. They were successful in getting onto a few key bidders' lists with large prospects that gave them access to significant opportunities via RFPs.

After engaging in several of these RFPs, it became clear that the cost of the pursuit was huge—but not only the financial cost. The principals quickly determined that credibly pursuing major deals also involves people—their own scarce human resources and their precious time. When their small team of very dedicated people became engaged in these complex pursuits, their talents were unavailable for other initiatives.

The biggest problem the team members faced was the inability to gauge the levels of risk in these larger deals. They had a great appetite and determination to win these opportunities with larger clients but no process to weave their way through the minefield of business issues tied to the deals. However, they were convinced that their technical delivery capability, proven through their portfolio of highly satisfied smaller clients, positioned them to take themselves to the next level.

RFP loss after RFP loss proved extremely frustrating. The firm's principals worried about the danger of taking on greater risk than they could bear in the interest of winning a deal. They just didn't know how to credibly evaluate which deals to pursue and which to avoid—and how to recognise and mitigate acceptable levels of risk.

We met with them at this crossroads in their evolution, and shared a proven, practical approach* to this type of issue. We helped the group at Top Tier understand the value of a set framework to help selling organisations make logical determinations about early exit or early acceleration in enterprise pursuits. Truthfully, there should be no grey area between the two. Accelerate or exit? That's the question all organisations face. But how do you know?

The framework for answering that vexing question for Top Tier and all selling organisations starts with having a clear understanding of what your firm does really well and what both an ideal client and a truly aligned opportunity look like. With organisational honesty driving clarity in those two areas, you then need a practical Go/No-Go process to evaluate the worthiness of enterprise opportunities.

The process works as follows: By breaking each opportunity's key issues into three workable categories—client issues, selling team issues, and financing/contract issues,** you can evaluate each issue as a team and determine the levels of stability or risk for each one. That's the key.

---

* This approach is explained in detail in the book, *Sandler Enterprise Selling.*

** For more information, see *Sandler Enterprise Selling*'s Pursuit Navigator® Tool.

For each issue, are you stable or is there risk? Remember the risk issues that created such confusion for Top Tier? What might some of them be? How about whether you have multi-level relationships in the account? Or whether you clearly understand who your competitors are and what their relationships are with the prospect firm? What about contractual guarantees, warranties, or penalties that will likely be involved? Do you understand all the implications and consequences?

For the risks you've candidly identified, you build pragmatic action plans to quickly mitigate those areas of doubt and uncertainty, acting as early as possible. Nothing good will come of ignoring a risk issue and delaying action. The meter is running, and, as Top Tier quickly discovered, all your resources are being drained.

This process drives real results for your risk mitigation efforts, which can actually involve candid discussions with the account. This will either reinforce your confidence in a deal or clarify the levels of danger and risk. In either case, you gain actionable information to drive decisions. Of course, some measure of risk is expected—but not risk that you don't evaluate, don't address, or don't attempt to mitigate.

Acceptable risk is your call, but you can't make that call credibly without clearly understanding consequences. There's no sense in burying your head in the sand. With pragmatic risk mitigation, you either increase your chances of winning or verify the No-Go decision. This, by the way, is exactly what is needed by anyone pursuing complex enterprise deals.

So, how did Top Tier proceed? Did learning the new process magically lead the company to a huge win?

Not exactly, but here's what it did do. It helped Top Tier identify and mitigate a key issue in a large opportunity with a global manufacturing firm. Having recognised that the company did not have the full range of capabilities to address the prospect's problem, instead of bidding and losing, Top Tier mitigated the risk. They partnered with two other firms, one of which acted as primary on the deal, and the combined partners won the business.

Top Tier, as a result, added £1.8 million annually for a three-year contract, roughly increasing their annual revenues by 50%. Was this the game changer they were seeking? For sure. Top Tier now understands the mantra of early exit or early acceleration. For them and for all selling organisations, these are both gifts.

Reflection

It takes time and effort to customise your sales process. Many amateur salespeople are too lazy to do this and are therefore destined to generate inconsistent and average sales results. The gold medal salesperson takes the time to build a customised, structured sales process, i.e., a sales template, and is rewarded with consistent, highly effective sales results. Remember Coach Wooden's wise words: "Your best is good enough. Don't beat yourself, don't cheat yourself, don't short-change yourself. That's the worst defeat you'll ever suffer, and you'll never get over it."

SALES MUSCLE #10

Your Daily Attitude/Behaviour Journal

"The road to the Olympics, leads to no city, no country. It goes far beyond New York or Moscow, ancient Greece or Nazi Germany. The road to the Olympics leads—in the end—to the best within us."

—Jesse Owens

JESSE OWENS is an Olympic legend among Olympic legends.

The American athlete won four Olympic gold medals in the 1936 Berlin Games, set a world record in the long jump that stood for 25 years, and was, as result of his success in those games, widely regarded as the greatest track and field star of his generation. He is best known, however, for single-handedly demolishing the reigning myth perpetuated by the Olympics' Nazi hosts that Hitler's Aryan athletes were superior to black competitors. Owens's four first-place finishes during the 1936 Games, an event that held immense propaganda implications for the Nazi regime, were inspiring to millions of people around the world who opposed Hitler's brutal racist ideology. After seeing Owens win the 100-metre sprint, an African-American journalist, Robert L. Vann, wrote:

> "And then...wonder of wonders...I saw Herr Adolph Hitler, salute this lad. I looked on with a heart which beat proudly as the lad who was crowned king of the 100 metres event, get an ovation the like of which I have never heard before. I saw Jesse Owens greeted by the Grand Chancellor of this country as a brilliant sun peeped out through the clouds. I saw a vast crowd of some 85,000 or 90,000 people stand up and cheer him to the echo."

As impressive and important as all of that is—and Owens's performance is among the most important events in Olympic history—the outcome of those contests are not as important, for our purposes, as the fact that Owens (according to *The Olympic Glory of Jesse Owens: A Contribution to Civil Rights and Society,* by Casey Aaron Nash) kept a daily diary as part of his training and preparation ritual prior to the Berlin Olympics. Like other gold medal athletes, Owens used journaling to keep track of what was working, what wasn't, and what needed improvement in his world.

Jesse Owens, arguably the most famous Olympian of all time, used a journal to keep track of what was most important in terms of his performance and his preparation.

As a gold medal salesperson, you should keep such a diary, too.

RELAX!

Please don't get spooked by the words "diary" and "journal." There is nothing scary about these words. Writing daily and focusing on your life and behaviour using the written word is an essential element of success. Externalising goals and actions brings into sharp focus what you are trying to achieve and the steps you need to perform to make these achievements a reality. Keeping track of your results helps you monitor your progress over time in a quantifiable way.

It sounds so simple, doesn't it? However, keeping a daily diary or journal is a discipline that low performers, average performers, and even a fair number of A-Players struggle to apply every day. What differentiates A-Players from the others is that no matter what they are faced with at the beginning of the day, A-Players know they need daily discipline to achieve their goals and ambitions. One way to track and measure that discipline is to create a daily Attitude/Behaviour Journal (A/B Journal). This is an essential conditioning trait of gold medal salespeople.

As mentioned earlier, amateur athletes typically play for fun and enjoyment. Thus the pressure to win is usually not extreme since the outcome of the game is unlikely to be the be-all and end-all for them. While amateur athletes may train and practice for a game or race, their daily activities are generally not centred around enhancing their sporting performance.

Gold medal athletes, in contrast, are the elite in their chosen field. They are focused and dedicated. Their entire day is systematically structured to enhance their sporting performance. A premier athlete will often train twice daily, or more, depending on the specific activity. The drive to attain peak performance and victory is the sole motivation of the elite athlete. Time, energy, and sacrifice are the daily disciplines of athletes participating at the highest level. They will wake up early and follow a strict dietary plan to provide the requisite fuel to power them through the grueling training they must endure to become the best. Of course, in addition they will formulate a daily plan.

Gold Medal Salespeople Know They Are Always on the Clock

As a gold medal salesperson, you have an obligation to create a daily plan, too. Think of it this way: "Your meter is always running."* This does not imply that you need to be prospecting or selling around the clock. However, it does mean that you approach every sales activity as an action that links to your sales goals. This begins with uncovering your motivation each and

* Source: *The Sandler Rules*, #29.

every day and creating a plan that you stick to so that you can navigate your path to success.

Creating an A/B Journal entry at the start of your day puts you into the right mindset to achieve your ambitions. Simply put, if you're a gold medal salesperson—or desire to be—it's what you do.

Gold medal salespeople know the value of time—that it is not to be wasted. Each action a person takes results in an outcome that is either positive or negative according to your perspective and present state of mind. This principle applies to all of your sales activities.

Amateur Salespeople Follow the Path of Least Resistance

How do amateur salespeople start their working day? Typically they roll out of bed, slump to the shower, suddenly realise it's later than they thought, dress maniacally, eat a rushed breakfast, and zoom to the office to start a flustered workday.

Once they arrive, amateur salespeople check their emails, leave the office to purchase a cup of coffee to shake off any lingering sleepiness, and then turn their attention to performing account-management tasks. All of the above activities take place before they begin any prospecting at all. Whether it is cold calling or following up with warm leads, amateur salespeople tend to avoid prospecting. Prospecting usually comes last on the list. Even though prospecting is the ticket to commissions, incentives, and increased cash in the bank, for the amateur salesperson the act of reaching out to an unknown person, with the aim of obtaining their money, is simply not a desirable to-do on the list.

The problem for amateur salespeople lies in their lack of motivation, or their non-alignment with what they are aiming to gain from their prospecting activities. The problem may also be a result of unsuccessful past experiences in selling their product or service. The path of least resistance may have become habitual through unhappy prospecting encounters. These could include being hung up on or worse after having called a prospect more than once. The amateur salesperson thinks proactive prospecting equates to being rude. Many salespeople have a store of awful gatekeeper or prospecting war stories.

Gold Medal Salespeople Write in a Journal Daily

A gold medal salesperson begins their day slightly differently from the amateur. Of course they wake up, wash, and eat their breakfast before they go to work. But it is what they do before they begin dialling or starting their selling activities that differentiates them from the amateur salesperson.

Gold medal salespeople take control of their actions, behaviour, and beliefs to shape the best results possible. How do they do this? They take responsibility for what they do, appreciate what is positive in their lives, and structure their day to maintain their focus and cultivate an A-Player mindset. Then, they make a list and put it in their A/B Journal.

Create Your Own Daily Attitude/Behaviour Journal

You too can choose to embark on this path (and follow Owens's example) by keeping an A/B Journal to take control of every working day.

Making this a consistent, daily practice yields optimum results. An ideal time to write up your journal entry is right before you begin looking at your emails in the morning. The initial weeks of maintaining your daily practice can be challenging. It can trigger your conscious (and subconscious) resistance to changing your negative or disempowering beliefs. But your daily journal is the "go-to" tool that allows you to optimise your daily activities.

Below is a template of an A/B Journal page.

Date:	**Daily Attitude/Behaviour Journal**
What I am grateful for	
What I want to attract	

Mindset affirmations	
What I commit to accomplishing today	
One goal to focus on today	
Why I want it	

Let's look in detail at what might go into an A/B Journal entry.

What I am grateful for

Here, list three to five things for which you are grateful to cultivate appreciation for the positive things in your life. It is important to be mindful when listing the things you are grateful for, which can vary from day to day. This practice of gratitude helps develop and foster an attitude of positivity and optimism.

What I want to attract

Here you list anything (and everything) that you are seeking to bring into your life. Put down anything you desire that is not presently in your life. The key is to not worry about how you will make it happen, but rather to focus on what you truly desire.

Mindset affirmations

Here you put down new beliefs that you want to bring into your life. These can include positive thoughts you hold about yourself, the service you provide, and the marketplace in which you work. You can use these ideas to replace your old beliefs that were limiting your progress.

Affirmations are based on the theory that what you believe creates your reality. The parallel principle is that your beliefs are what drive your behaviour. This in turn sets the bar for what you will and won't do.

What I commit to accomplishing today

Confidence and belief in yourself are generally considered the key determinants of whether you achieve your goals or not, in particular your sales goals. When you do 100% of what you say you will do, you build up your self-esteem. When you don't do what you say you will do, you chip away and deplete your self-esteem.

One goal to focus on today

What is recorded in this section of the A/B Journal acts as a laser beam to create the focus to keep you aligned with the bigger picture: the goal that you envision as your future. This goal is a core element within your daily journal that helps to raise your level of motivation each day.

Why I want it

Here, you can cement a deep emotional connection to your goal in order to motivate yourself through your internal resistance and comfort zones when these arise—and they will! The act of writing down why you want your goals every day grounds this affirmation, making this goal truly yours, while simultaneously strengthening your commitment muscle.

It takes 90 days to instill any new behaviour and create new patterns in our lives. So stick with it. The results will be life changing.

Examples of Daily Attitude/Behaviour Journals

A/B Journal: Joel, Business Development Exec, Tech Startup

Wednesday, March 15

What I am grateful for

- Allison. Always.
- Raju—for quickly resolving coding issue with the off-shore team yesterday before lag time became critical.
- Booked meeting with Simon Graham.
- Great call with Ian—he's interested!
- Prospecting plan now in motion.
- Good initial reviews for landing page mockup.
- My family and friends.

What I want to attract

- A-Player performances from Steven and Robert.

- More businesses like Silver Beam, who know that we're better than what they have, appreciate and value that, and are willing to invest in their IT.
- £150K in new business.
- My dream board, all of it—no excuses!

Mindset affirmations

- Great sales KPIs demonstrate a fantastic opportunity to grow.
- Things aren't happening due to "luck" or being in the right place at the right time; I'm controlling the process and making the sales.
- My "I" is constantly 10.

What I commit to accomplishing today

- Prep investor account meeting.
- Last amends to WCID proposal.
- Active listening in Gola meeting today.
- Set up-front contracts for meeting with Jazar.
- Set up integration meeting with GoCubed for Friday.
- Finalise sales budget with Peter Martin.

One goal to focus on today

- Consistent "I"-10 rating!

Why I want it

- When I'm in a good place, everything goes better.

A/B Journal: Rashad, Client Services Manager, Health Insurance company

Thursday, February 16

What I am grateful for

- Up for facing my demon head trash!
- LinkedIn strategy finally set up!
- Goldstone for appreciating our honesty and expertise, really cool to find oneself in the trusted advisor position.
- 1-2-1 with GF today.
- Good sales meeting yesterday.
- Roman for trusting me with this role; I hope it's starting to pay off!
- Having a big weekend planned with my best friend, and Monday off for a break.

What I want to attract

- For this year to be the breakthrough year in all areas of my life.
- Great clients who are willing to work with us, not have us work for them.
- Close out Investec and SABB by end of Q1 January for *yesses*.
- More, as this attracts more—a positive thought process that we can achieve our wildest dreams.
- Good health for me and my family and friends.

- Have a great call with Simon Blaine tomorrow and close out as per my proposal this month and new year contract signed this year.

Mindset affirmations

- Other people's opinions of me are none of my business.
- I'm the best person for this role.
- My yearly goals are deliverable with ease and fun!
- My destiny is in my own hands.
- I deserve and accept the very best in all areas of my life, and my hard work, dedication, and SMART plans and actions ensure I achieve all my dreams and goals.

What I commit to accomplishing today

- Phone yesterday's non-attendees.
- Attend Expand London networking event this evening.
- Review my prospecting plan to go over it with my Sandler coach next week.
- Sort out contracts for EM.
- Get to the gym after work today!

One goal to focus on today

- Signing 200 users by the end of the year.

Why I want it

- Sets me up to smash my sales KPIs for this year.

Case Study: Anne's Experience after 90 Days Writing an A/B Journal

Anne, a technical writer, wrote about her experience with a daily journal.

"I've always been motivated to achieve big things. That's never been a problem. However, before starting to do an A/B Journal, I was most motivated to accomplish great goals, often at the beginning of a new year. While I'd make plans to accomplish many things on January 1, without fail after a few weeks I'd abandoned many of them or even forgotten that I'd wanted to achieve them.

"The notion of the A/B Journal appealed to me because it meant setting smaller goals, ones I was much more likely to accomplish. It freed me from trying to accomplish everything and instead helped me focus on accomplishing the most important things.

"Very soon after I committed to this daily practice, I found that setting daily goals forced me to think in terms of concrete action steps, rather than just lofty plans. It got me moving towards my long-term goals on a daily basis.

"I set no more than four daily goals at a time, which taught me how to prioritise. I learned how to set mini-goals, with the new understanding that daily goals must be limited in time. I related these mini-goals to my finances, health, relationships, or other areas of my life. Because they were doable, I was able to increase the likelihood of accomplishing them and was making progress toward my larger goals at the same time.

"The practice of doing the daily journal was a routine that empowered me to accomplish bigger things. It created a momentum that took me forward by consistently succeeding at small things every day. Some of my mini-goals have become daily habits, like doing some form of meditation every day.

"Maintaining my daily practice certainly wasn't easy—especially sticking to my commitment of doing it for 90 days every day. Some days I really didn't want to do it. There would be days when it took me a really long time to complete it.

"Among the things that really worked for me were the different components of the journal. The fact that I had to come up with five things that I'm grateful for every day was a fantastic way of focusing on what I did have in my life, rather than what I didn't have. This generated a more positive mindset in me about life in general.

"What I wanted to attract was also a really interesting section because as well as the things I wanted to attract, like better relationships, there were also things that I internally set myself to attract, such as more resilience and more self-esteem. This became a powerful tool of personal growth for me.

"The mindset affirmations section also benefited me greatly. When I started doing my daily journal, I found it difficult to actually identify the negative thoughts that were running (and ruining!) my life. They were buried underneath my conscious thoughts. However, when I got going, sticking with this was nothing short of transformational. Uncovering my self-limiting beliefs (which sometimes I had to sit with for up to five minutes to uncover) brought the thoughts into the light, so to speak. What is truly amazing is the words that came out of me for the mindset affirmations. What emerged were not only powerful, affirming words, but also affirmations that were actually action-based—intuitive strategies that added weight and substance to these affirming words."

Reflection

Attitude is usually the most important attribute for sales success. A person's attitude can vary from minute to minute, hour to hour, day to day. Gold medal salespeople realise they need to start their day with a very powerful and resilient attitude. The practice of writing a daily Attitude/Behaviour Journal before checking emails ensures that the day starts with your attitude in the right place. Moreover, the practice of writing a daily journal builds a powerful, attitudinal muscle that impacts positively and powerfully on all areas of your life.

EPILOGUE

The Power of Reinforcement

WHEN IT COMES to improving your sales muscles, think of making this a way of life, not a one-time event.

This book is for those people who choose to achieve their goals. Use the sales approach outlined in this book in all your sales and prospecting activities.

The preceding chapters have dealt with the importance of goal setting and becoming truly connected to personal aspirations to motivate you on your journey to success, describing the process to create your tailored plan and daily activity to make your long-term ambitions a reality.

Gold medal salespeople know that the way to continue to thrive and be successful is to continue learning and honing their craft. Staying engaged in ongoing improvement and utilising the support systems of like-minded sales professionals ensures that you can keep progressing, confident that you will hit the benchmarks you set and enjoy the rewards. The biggest lesson to be learned is that you will never stop learning. The future is bright and uncertain; therefore, to be best prepared, it is important to be open to novel methods. The foundation of a win-win no-pressure approach, with clear up-front contracts, remains the best sales framework to implement in prospecting and sales activities. If you are not using this approach, it is time for a change. Even as financial markets are prone to development and change, gold medal salespeople must also be prepared to change.

Gold medal athletes do not attend week-long workshops and pronounce that they are now experts in the field. No serious person has ever finished a five-day track and field training programme and said that they have now learned everything they need to win the Olympic decathlon. In the same vein, amateur salespeople who attend a two-day cold-calling course or a day's seminar on digital marketing and prospecting techniques and then believe that they have acquired the knowledge and experience to be the best salesperson possible are fooling themselves. To master any skill, what is required is the diligent learning of applicable theory and material that is practiced in the real world daily and over time.

Are you committed to your personal sales success? Do you have systems and a structured plan in place with which to achieve it? Those who have taken the time to read this book have already proven they are dedicated to achieving their professional goals and ambitions, so, if you are among them, you too have what it takes to succeed.

The path to your desired destination will not always be easy, especially in the world of professional sales. There will be many more *noes* than *yesses*, and you will have to prospect consistently and effectively to push through your comfort zones daily. But if you are committed to living the life you wish to live, the struggle is a given and is integral to your development as a gold medal salesperson.

Now, flex those muscles, start conditioning yourself, and set yourself up to win!

Look for these other books on shop.sandler.com:

SALES SERIES

The Art and Skill of Sales Psychology
Asking Questions the Sandler Way
Bootstrap Selling the Sandler Way
Call Center Success the Sandler Way
Digital Prospecting
The Contrarian Salesperson
LinkedIn the Sandler Way
Prospect the Sandler Way
Retail Success in an Online World
Sandler Enterprise Selling
The Sandler Rules
The Unapologetic Saleswoman
Why People Buy
You Can't Teach a Kid to Ride a Bike at a Seminar

MANAGEMENT SERIES

Change the Sandler Way
Customer Service the Sandler Way
Lead When You Dance
Motivational Management the Sandler Way
Misery to Mastery
The Intentional Sales Manager
The Right Hire
The Road to Excellence
The Sales Coach's Playbook
The Sandler Rules for Sales Leaders
The Success Cadence
Transforming Leaders the Sandler Way
Winning from Failing

MOTIVATIONAL SERIES

Accountability the Sandler Way
From the Board Room to the Living Room
Sandler Success Principles
Succeed the Sandler Way

INDUSTRY SERIES

Making Channel Sales Work
Patient Care the Sandler Way
Selling in Manufacturing and Logistics
Selling Professional Services the Sandler Way
Selling to Homeowners the Sandler Way
Selling Technology the Sandler Way